Andrew Lang

The Politics of Aristotle

Introductory Essays

Andrew Lang

The Politics of Aristotle
Introductory Essays

ISBN/EAN: 9783337073657

Printed in Europe, USA, Canada, Australia, Japan

Cover: Foto ©Thomas Meinert / pixelio.de

More available books at **www.hansebooks.com**

LONDON

LONGMANS, GREEN, AND CO.

1880

CONTENTS.

INTRODUCTORY NOTES.

I.

THE 'POLITICS' OF ARISTOTLE.

THE POLITICS of Aristotle have a double value: they contain the first really scientific discussion of the origin, the elements, the constitution, and the conditions of human society, and they are a storehouse of information as to the facts of the history of Greece. It is true that conscious reflection on the different shapes and possible perfect form of the State, on its relations to the Individual, and on its international rights and duties, had been awake in Greece long before the age of Aristotle. The great questions had been propounded and discussed, the terminology had been almost fixed. In the first place had arisen the early Lawgivers, Solon, Charondas, Zaleucus, Philolaus—whom we may call the Judges—and the early mystics, Pythagoras, Apollo's son, Epimenides, the healer of souls, and Empedocles, who were in a sense the Prophets of Hellas. The latter possessed a secret of life, a certain method of conduct, which they inculcated to disciples, who then formed small communities within the cities of Sicily and Italy.

B

From these mystics Aristotle received, through tradition, many ideas, and, above all, the notion of the power
which the lawgiver has to direct the conduct of men to
a moral end. From the example of the great Spartan
lawgiver Lycurgus, whom the Delphian Pythoness knew
not whether to address as God or as mortal, and from
the enduring influence which his system of almost
monastic discipline exercised on Sparta, Aristotle, like
other Greek writers on politics, drew the conclusion
that one man of impressive character, backed by the
influence of religion, might mould the characters of men
to a uniform type. Hence the recurrent idea of the
Lawgiver (νομοθέτης) who, with the help of the Delphian
oracle, is to fashion the spiritual lives of the citizens
towards a given end. Again, the Lawgivers who appear
on the horizon of really historical times, such as Solon,
had codified and committed to writing the unwritten
customs and dooms of early Greece; and the ideas fixed
in these customs and dooms, ideas dating from the time
when the Chieftain-Priest was a living oracle of law,
greatly coloured the political speculations of Aristotle.

After the actual legislators came the amateur
theorists, like Phaleas and Hippodamus, who seem to
have tried, in a fashion, to buttress the old traditional
notions of Greece, with the help of the new rational
doctrines, which we connect with the names of the
earlier sophists.

Still later appeared the wandering rhetoricians, disturbing the repose of political custom, with arguments
drawn from abstract notions about Right, Virtue,
Nature, Law, and so forth. These arguments were

popularised by dramatists like Euripides, who made his characters speculate on duty and morality on the stage, and who did for the new democracies what Pindar and Theognis had done for the ancestral aristocracies—gave them poetic texts in support of their ideas. Next Plato, in a variety of dialogues, had sought after some permanent basis for morality, had constructed an ideal state, had discussed almost every difficulty which Aristotle handles, and one may almost say had left, in beautiful scattered fragments, the notions which Aristotle tries to arrange into a scientific body of doctrine. Plato had amplified the teaching of Socrates, and had helped out reason by imagination, by rhetoric, and by the invention of myths, which like the gods in the plays appear whenever there is a *nodus vindice dignus*. Xenophon had discussed the constitution of Sparta with partisan admiration, and had treated of the commercial democracy of Athens, and pointed out the way to make her more wealthy and indolent than ever, with the irony of a man of high birth and education, a soldier and a sportsman. Acquainted, as we may believe, with all or most of these writings, and with the political thought of Thucydides, and not uninfluenced by any of them, Aristotle went to work to build up a philosophy of human society, which should neither depend wholly on old traditional wisdom, nor be a series of empirical maxims, a *moyen de parvenir* in politics, nor rest upon poetic imagination; but should be founded on a collection of facts, and on the teaching of historical experience. Quite

unlike Plato, he determined to discard no institution—
as the Family, and Property—which immemorial use
approved. He would introduce nothing new, nothing
which had to be based on a myth, for he probably
perceived that myths had been invented to account for
institutions already sacred, and that no new custom
could be made sacred by being grounded on an equally
new myth. Thus he neither rejects anything dear to
men (ἀγαπητόν) from of old, nor brings in a new
ἀγαπητόν, like the Enthusiasm of Humanity.

II.

ARISTOTLE'S CONCEPTION OF POLITICAL SCIENCE.

BEFORE entering on the study of Aristotle's scientific
philosophy of the State, it may be well to ask what he
meant by his science; and further, whether he was
mistaken in thinking that a science of Politics is possible
at all. Now if by political science be understood a
knowledge of the general laws of human nature, acting
in political associations, and of the effects of variable
causes, such as the influence of great men, sufficient to
enable the philosopher to predict, and if he chooses to
alter the development of history, we may say that Aristotle did not consider this science possible, and did not
attempt to construct it. If he had made any such preten-
sions his own failure would be obvious. He lived in an
age of slavery, and far from foretelling a day when slavery

should fall into discredit and disuse, he gave it a place
among the ' *natural* ' institutions of society, such as
property and the family, and left it there. He lived
in a country of small city states, and in a time when
the spirit of these states had departed, when their
liberty had well-nigh perished, and he proposed no
scheme of union, and looked forward to no such fresh
order of things as the Roman Empire, or the national
system of modern Europe, or even to such a federation
as the Achæan League. Such a new and striking
factor in politics as the beginning of the Macedonian
Empire seems to attract his attention indeed, but gets
no notice in detail. Again, although the military age
of Greece was practically past, he did his best to dis-
courage industrial development, and left a stigma on
commerce and on credit which still clings to them.
What, then, did Aristotle mean by ἡ πολιτική—political
science? What was his idea of its scope, its aim, and
its method? In the first place, he gives this science
the loftiest rank in the hierarchy of sciences; it is ἡ
κυριωτάτη καὶ μάλιστα ἀρχιτεκτονική.[1]
Political science takes this lofty place, because the
matter which it deals with is the noblest. That matter is
the nature of Man, and of Man too in his highest relations, in the conditions within which alone he attains
his most perfect, his almost divine development,
namely, as the free citizen of a free state. The end of
this science is like that of all sciences—the attainment
of good, but of good in its brightest form, the form of
Justice.[2] Now Justice here is only another name for the

[1] Ethics, i. 2, 5.   [2] Pol. iii. 12, 1.

common weal ; or, in other words, the end of political
science is to discover the conditions under which every
citizen will be able to secure the most free and perfect
development of himself, consistent with the good of the
State, without impediment in harmonious circumstances.
But as this ideal harmony of circumstances is not always
to be found, it is the practical duty of political science to
study the almost infinite diversity of existing circumstances, 'for there is not one sort of democracy or one
sort of oligarchy only,' and to suggest the adaptation
of institutions to facts which have come into existence
through different laws of historical necessity.[3] Laws
must be made for states, not states for laws. Therefore
untiring study and collection of *facts* are necessary. The
nature of political science, and its scope, as conceived
of by Aristotle, are now apparent. It is the science
which observes man in the sum of his relations, as
historically exhibited in his institutions. It is a science
based on the collection of facts, and on the discrimina-
tion of countless shades and gradations in the evolution
of the various forms of government. And it is the
science which, having thus obtained a clear and critical
conception of man's needs and powers, applies that
conception to his institutions, and attempts to bring
them into harmony with circumstances. Again, it is
the science which constructs, as a type and example, a
model of the ideal state in which men might reach
perfection, if perfection could ever be reached by more
than an isolated person, here and there in the world.
Sometimes the brightness of this ideal conception blinds

[3] Pol. iv. 1, 11.

Aristotle to the value of the ordinary civic life of
Greece, and draws him away from realities. But
Aristotle always has history and historical development
present to his mind; he has a fact for every assertion;
he is keenly alive to the immense variety, the many
differences in institutions which come under the same
general name, such as Democracy, Liberty, Tyranny,
and so on. It is in his continual reference to history
and to fact that he is most instructive. His collection
of the constitutions of one hundred and fifty-eight
Greek states, and his researches into the customs of
barbarous tribes, with his habit of making these customs
throw light on the earlier institutions of Greece, give him
a place among students of what we now call Comparative Politics. Aristotle is not satisfied with saying, like
one of the characters in Plato's ' Republic,' that ' there
are reported to be many and absurd forms of government among barbarians.' He notes the constitutional
kingship of the Molossi; he remarks on an early Greek
custom like compurgation; on the fact that the Greeks
used to buy their wives from each other; and he mentions some curious traits of savage manners.[4] Thus
Aristotle studied political life in the spirit of modern
criticism, and he treated many modern problems in a
scientific fashion. But his science has many preconceptions and prejudices, his method many peculiarities,
his field of observation many necessary limits; and all
these combine to make him seem remote, out of date,
and difficult of comprehension to modern readers'
It is therefore needful first to give an account of

[4] Rep. 544; Pol. v. 10, 8; vii. 2, 11; ii. 8, 20.

Aristotle's Method, and of his preconceptions, and then
to trace in history the development of the Greek City-
state to which his speculation is confined.

III.

ON SOME LEADING CONCEPTIONS OF ARISTOTLE.

In reading the 'Politics' of Aristotle we meet with many
arguments which appear either to want force altogether,
or to depend for their force on some conception not
stated, or on some premise taken for granted as if it
were generally known and admitted by everyone.
There seems to be a store of ideas in the background,
which no one is expected to dispute, and which Aristotle
appeals to with confidence. When he has brought a
theory within the reach of one of these conceptions,
such as Nature, Measure, the End, Order, he is satisfied
that he has made his point. Some of these conceptions
are tolerably familiar to us, others less familiar, or even
strange ; some of them are parts of Aristotle's general
system, for it must never be forgotten that his 'Politics'
is only one stone, a corner-stone, in a whole theory of
knowledge ; some, again, may be called Greek common-
places, notions that were parcels of the mind of Greece ;
and some are part of Aristotle's inheritance from the
older philosophers, such as Pythagoras and Anaxagoras.
Then there are processes of argument which do not
seem always convincing to us, especially the argument
from the analogy of the arts, with conclusions in the

sphere of politics. Again, there is a strong belief in the power of the Legislators, to whom the Greeks were wont to attribute such arrangements as the συσσίτια,—the early distributions of land, and so on— arrangements which we believe to have been produced by circumstances, before the age of law, out of the remains of tribal customs. Further, there is the tendency in Aristotle which we may almost call mystic —the tendency to look now to an ideal life of political virtue, now to an ideal life of philosophic contemplation, or to a blending of both, as the best for individuals and for the State. Besides all this, there is the obscurity arising from a method of arguing in which ἀπορίαι, or difficulties, are put forward, while the question is not definitely settled, but is relegated to some later portion of the 'Politics.'

On the whole the method of Aristotle may be called analytical, with a view to a later synthesis. He will examine the ultimate units, the elements of every compound existence, before pronouncing on the nature of the whole which the elements make up.[5] In the 'Organon' and in the 'Ethics' he has analysed the psychological and moral elements in the nature of the Individual ; and in the 'Politics' he begins by examining the component elements and the conditions of the State, as husband and wife, father and children, master and slave, owner and property, citizens of this rank and citizens of that lower grade, as differentiated by such natural causes as birth, wealth, occupation. But all the time that he is analysing, Aristotle has present to his mind some very dis-

[5] Pol. i. 2, 1.

tinct ideas as to the nature of the whole, as to the natural, unspoiled form of the State. These ideas are the result of all sorts of factors, of aristocratic prejudice, of traditional morality, and of a philosophic theory about Nature, which it is necessary to understand.

Aristotle mentions among the devices of Sophists the trick of ringing changes on the terms Nature, and Law, or Conventional Institutions. The dialecticians of Greece had discovered that ' the estimates of things just and honourable, with which Political Science is concerned, shift and vary so much, as to seem the result of capricious enactment, rather than of Nature.'[6] In fact the revolutionary thinkers of Greece laid much the same stress on Nature (meaning thereby the presumed primitive freedom from all authority of law, reason, and custom) as Rousseau did in his ' Discourses on the Origin of Inequality among Men.' This is a common sort of reaction against a complicated civilisation, founded on religious and traditional beliefs which men have ceased to believe in. Now the purpose of Aristotle was conservative, and thus it became his object to prove that the institutions he wished to preserve were not the result of capricious enactment, but were founded on Nature. But Aristotle's way of understanding Nature is just the reverse of Rousseau's way, except when it suits his purpose to shift his ground, as in the disquisition on money and trade. Nature is identical with the fulfilment, and final cause of all progress to an end ($\dot{\eta}$ δὲ φύσις τέλος καὶ οὗ ἕνεκα).[7] Nature is matter fully fashioned and elaborated rather than matter in the rough (μᾶλλον αὐτὴ φύσις τῆς ὕλης).

---

[6] Ethics, i. 3, 2.   [7] Nat. Auscult. ii. 1, 10.

Man in a state of Nature is Man as Nature would have him to be, that is, as Aristotle would have him to be, a free warrior, statesman, and politician, at leisure, not a savage, feeding on acorns. ' Nature seeks not only right activity, but the power of living in noble leisure.' Contrast this with Rousseau's State of Nature : ' L'exemple des sauvages qu'on a presque tous trouvés à ce point, semble confirmer que le genre humain étoit fait pour y rester toujours. . . . et que tous les progrès ultérieurs ont été en apparence autant de pas vers la perfection de l'individu, et en effet, vers la décrépitude de l'espèce.' [8] The contrast is particularly marked where Rousseau denounces the man who invented property, which Aristotle declares to be an institution suggested by Nature and ' unspeakably sweet.' [9]

In Aristotle's eyes, then, Nature is almost the unconscious action of the will of the world, bringing all things into uniformity with limit and with right reason. The right reason of course is Aristotle's notion of what is best. Mr. Grote's way of stating the doctrine of Nature makes the matter very clear, if we apply to politics what is said of physics and metaphysics. ' There are in the sublunary bodies ' (in which form is implicated with matter) ' both constant tendencies and variable tendencies. The *constant* Aristotle calls "Nature," which always aspire to Good, or to the renovation of Forms as perfect as may be, though impeded in this work by adverse influences, and therefore never producing anything but individuals comparatively

[8] Discours sur l'origine de l'inégalité parmi les hommes.
[9] Pol. ii. 5, 8.

defective, and sure to perish. The *variable* tendencies
he calls Spontaneity and Chance, always modifying, dis-
torting, frustrating the full purposes of Nature.' [10]
If we apply this doctrine to politics, we find that the
matter is human character, and human circumstance,
which *Nature* fashions into the forms of the family and
the state. The *constant* tendencies in human character
and circumstance make for good and for order. Such
a tendency is that which keeps all things in due subordination of ruler and subject, which sets father over
child, master over slave, old over young, reason over
passion, which makes the city *wish* to consist of equals,
which when one man or one family is undeniably
better than the rest, as gods are better than men, puts
kingly or aristocratic rule into their hands. Thus the
results of Nature's unchecked workings are the *Family*,
with due subordination of woman, child, and slave ;
the *Monarchy*, with due obedience to the one Godlike
man, who alone contributes more to the stock of excellence than all the others ; the *Aristocracy*, where a few
are equally pre-eminent ; and the *Polity*, where there
is a natural equality among the citizens. In all these
natural forms of rule government is exercised in the
interest of the natural *whole*, the State and citizens.
On the other side are *variable* tendencies, *contrary* to
Nature, which ruin the subordination of families, which
induce men to take money, a mere *instrument*, for the
end of their life, which work for the overthrow of
natural slavery, which drive the one best man or the
one best family out of the cities, which prevent the

[10] Grote, Aristotle, i. 165.

State from consisting of equals, which, in short, produce
these abnormal and unnatural distortions called *tyrannies, democracies,* and *oligarchies,* which govern in the
interest of an overgrown member of the whole. Thus
Nature is always being frustrated and defeated, and
from this point of view Aristotle's doctrine of the
decline of states is not so very far removed from the
scheme of Plato, with its fatal cycles of better and
worse.

Analogous to the idea of Nature in Aristotle is the
idea of the limit, τὸ πέρας, and of τὸ πεπερασμένον, the
finite. Both these notions seem to be derived from the
Pythagorean catalogue of limit and limitless, odd and
even, one and many, good and bad, male and female,
and the rest, which became a sort of accepted canon
with Greek thinkers.

Limit and the infinite are the elements out of which
the orderly and knowable world is made. The infinite
is all disorder, confusion, a blur of undistinguishable
sensations, and in morals of masterless passions, till, by
the introduction of the limit, chaos is slowly made
orderly, and passions are formed into character. Apply-
ing, for instance, this conception to the question, is commerce a legitimate occupation? Aristotle answers no, because οὐδὲν δοκεῖ πέρας εἶναι πλούτου καὶ κτήσεως, there
is no necessary *limit* to the acquisition of wealth.[11] Now
wealth is defined to be abundance of the instruments
necessary towards the independent life. These used
to be obtained by barter, and a man was satisfied
when he had enough of them, that sufficiency was the

[11] Pol. i. 9, 1.

πέρας. But when money was invented, and it was commonly held that wealth meant abundance of money, there was no natural πέρας to the acquisition of coin, ἄπειρος δὴ οὗτος ὁ πλοῦτος. But there is a deeper reason than this for the fact that the endless acquisition of wealth is unnatural. Desire of riches springs from that character which thirsts insatiably for life, not for the noble life, which seeks satisfaction in the chaotic and infinite field of pleasure, without definite end, not in striving after the limit and end of existence.[12] Here the *limit* (πέρας), from another point of view becomes identical with the *end* and aim of life (the τέλος). This τέλος is the same for the State and for the individual, namely, happiness. No conception is more constantly in Aristotle's mind than this of the End. From all past experience and history he has arrived at a fixed and luminous idea of what Nature would have, what all her workings tend to. This is not the life of men wandering in nomadic hordes, nor of men living as husbandmen in scattered villages, nor of great servile nations. The free wild tribes of the North have no central engrossing interest and bond of life ; the peoples of Asia are gifted with intellect and art, but they are slavish. Hellas alone occupies the happy mean, alone offers to men in the city-state an object for noble action that must fill all their lives, and an environment of free relationships in which to exercise virtue. The State is the *limit*, beyond which Nature does not wish to pass in the formation of political organisms. The State in its perfection and the citizen in perfection are

[12] Pol. i. 9, 17 ; Plato, Laws, 714.

the *end* of her travail. Now that perfection is happiness. But is the happiness to be that of practical activity and the exercise of moral virtue, or that of philosophical contemplation?

The consideration of the τέλος thus brings us to what is a standing difficulty in reading Aristotle. He seems to hesitate whether to recommend a possible life of civic virtue and activity, or an ideal life of contemplation to men and states. The latter life answers to the saintly life, the entrance into ' religion ;' the former corresponds to the knightly life of the Middle Ages. As we have within us, he seems to say, the power of raising some divine element to a momentary delight in the divine reason, a momentary recognition of our connection with divinity, ought we not to make this our τέλος ? Can this contemplative existence be combined with the political existence ? This is the question which is treated in the book on the Ideal State. It is here, then, that the mystic element appears amid the common sense and historical activity of Aristotle. Indeed, when we come to analyse his method, we find three incongruous elements, really scientific enquiry, aristocratic prejudice, and the dreams of a metaphysic which literally *sublimi ferit sidera vertice,* and listens for the eternal harmonies of Nature.

IV.

THE GREEK CITY-STATE.

THE political speculations of Aristotle are bounded by the limits of the πόλις, or City-state, which he looks on as the ultimate and perfect form of society.[13] It does not seem to have occurred to him, who, in his literary criticism, was ready to admit that the Drama might advance in changed circumstances to new forms, that human society also might come to be fixed on a wider basis than the city—on the basis, namely, of the nation. The political unit with which he concerned himself, the town of perhaps ten or fifteen thousand free citizens, supported by slave-labour, enjoying a life of leisure and culture, self-ruled, and exercising all the rights of a sovereign state, was the form of society through which Greece attained her eminence in war, and in the arts. It was therefore his business to understand all the conditions which contributed to make up the City-state, to point out the causes which in the past had frustrated its development, and had sometimes perverted it from being the home of noble life into the seat of Tyranny, of Oligarchy, of Sedition, of the later Democracy, ignoble in the eyes of Aristotle. The ideal aim of the State was to give room and opportunity for the full and free development of the best powers of all its citizens; that aim, as conceived of by the philosophers, had never been actually reached. Here, of

[13] Pol. i. 2, 8.

course, we touch the point where Aristotle's political speculation diverges from that of later times. Modern thought is concerned with nations, that is with what were originally ἔθνη, aggregates of tribes with no political unity in the Greek sense. Various causes have united the descendants of these tribes into the large associations which we call nations. The common possession of conquered lands by a tribe of kin; the defeat of one tribe by another, with the retention of its freedom under the new over-lord; the unity imposed by the Church; the dislike of city life; the growth of kingly power, which could not well grow in a city; all these, with other causes, have brought about a wider and looser organisation than that of the city. But all Aristotle's thought is conditioned by the existence of the city, which had so powerful an attraction for the Greeks, and which, within its narrow bounds, could actually school them in morality, and in the spiritual life. To do this is, of course, beyond the power of a national government, and thus Aristotle's ideas are in a different plane from that occupied by modern speculation.

To understand the conditions under which the City-state grew up, out of general laws which were everywhere the same, and everywhere checked and diverted by varying causes, it is necessary to look back to the dawn of Greek history. The State, as Aristotle knew it, was 'the inevitable consequence of its antecedents in the past,' and Aristotle himself enables us to trace a sketch of these antecedents. The State (Πόλις) is ἡ τοῦ εὖ ζῆν κοινωνία καὶ ταῖς οἰκίαις καὶ τοῖς γένεσι ζωῆς τελείας χάριν καὶ αὐτάρκους, 'an association of families and clans in a higher life for the sake of a perfect and self-sufficing existence.'[14] It is thus that Aristotle adds to the bare facts, the union of villages, a moral interpretation. This union was not without the will of Nature, which was leading men towards the perfect life. His aim is to be a fellow-worker with Nature, by pointing out the faults of human character which retard the advance to perfection in Nature's political school, the City.

When the tribes, which came in time to develop Hellenic civilisation, were first settling in Hellas, when they were invading the country from the North, or landing in her ports from the East, they were not yet, it may be said with some certainty, what Aristotle would have considered actually political beings. They lived in scattered villages κατὰ κώμας, and it may be presumed that their society was based, not on the πόλις of course, but on the group, γένος, and on the family, οἰκία. Their lands were probably held on a communal system—that is to say, if we may judge by analogy and by traces of institutions, they were not the property of individuals, but of village groups of men (γένη), united by the belief in descent from a common ancestor, and by the practice of certain religious sacrifices in common. This is a primitive stage of society which is found to have existed in most parts of the world—a stage in society which takes no notice of the individual as such, but merely of the group, or γένος. It is the γένος which is wronged if one of the group be slain or injured ; it is the γένος which inherits property, and is responsible for the actions of each of the individuals within its circle.

[14] Pol. iii. 9, 12.

This formed a stage in the development of the English race too, but the difference began when the Greeks had once tasted of city life, which satisfied them so thoroughly that they never sought a wider unity. On the other hand, the wider national unity was imposed on the English before they came to care for city life. To take another instance. It was the misfortune of the Irish Celts that they lived under the clan system, with only abortive attempts at a wider unity, till conquerors came among them to whom the clan system seemed an abomination. But this primitive condition of things had ceased to exist in most of the states that made up Hellas before regular history begins : it had ceased to exist, in all its simplicity and vigour, as soon as several γένη deserted their villages, or at least removed the shrine of their religions, and their place of meeting, to some central spot, where their nobler families began to dwell within the walls of a city, and on the crest of some commanding hill. (This process of clustering together, and of combining several clans, with their religions, was called ϕυνοίκισις, and was generally attributed to the initiative of some primitive king, or hero, or demigod. With the συνοίκισις of villages, the Greek city was born, and only Attica was fortunate enough to be the scene of the perfect συνοίκισις of many cities, into the great city of Athens. By the process a new sort of life, a higher life, τὸ εὖ ζῆν, began for the clansmen. Their tribal hero, father and lord long dead, or their tribal fetich, was no longer their highest conception in religion. Their sacred clan-festivals still existed, but in subordination to the loftier and purer creed which became common to them all. The members of the various clans, sons of Æacus or of Eumolpus, recognised each other as kindred by an older descent; they were all γεννῆται 'Απόλλωνος πατρῷου, brothers together in Apollo, and Zeus of the household guarded each man's home and enclosure.[15] Thus the newer faith succeeded the old without a break in continuity; it was still ancestor-worship, only of a father more remote and powerful. With his cultus comes a wider morality than that of the tribe. If a man is slain, the slayer falls under the wrath of Apollo, and of the State as well as of the clan. He cannot escape by paying a blood-fine (ποινή, wer-gild, eric) to the clan or kindred of his victim, or braving their vendetta. The Greeks found, as the Basutos in Africa find to-day, that, 'if they avenged themselves, the town would soon be dispersed.'[16]

Thus a nobler religion, a wider and purer morality, a more settled body of customary law, laid down by the Chieftains of the old clans, τὸ εὖ ζῆν in fact, began with the allegiance to the city. But it did not follow that, because the State had become the ruling idea, and the State-god the main religious conception, and because the life of individuals was partly emancipated from the solidarité of the clan, it did not follow that the clan became extinct. It survived in a modified shape, and was one of the most powerful factors in building the new constitution, and the State as known to Aristotle. The history of a Greek city is to a very great extent the history

---

[15] Plato, Luthydemus, 302. Harpokration. 'Απόλλων πατρῷος ὁ Πύθιος. τὸν δὲ 'Απόλλωνα κοινῶς πατρῷον τιμῶσιν 'Αθηναῖοι ἀπὸ Ἴωνος, τούτου γὰρ οἰκίσαντος τὴν 'Αττικήν, ὡς 'Αριστοτέλης φησί, τοὺς 'Αθηναίους Ἴωνας κληθῆναι, καὶ 'Απόλλω πατρῷον αὐτοῖς ὀνομασθῆναι.

[1] E. B. Tylor, *Contemporary Review*, June 1873.

of the struggle waged by the chief and most wealthy
families within the clans, the dwellers in the *city*, in
whose veins the clan's blood ran purest, against the
body of the *rustic* clansmen, and probably against the
later immigrants, the broken men from other tribes, who
were attracted by every growing centre of settled life.[17]
The chiefs (βασιλικὸν γένος) claimed from old time
that power 'to make foul weather or fair,' which the
Brehon laws attributed to Irish chieftains.[18] They had
exclusive privileges, knew the law, or were inspired to
deliver it, and they alone could keep up that unbroken
practice of religious rites on which all the luck of
the community was believed to turn. The common
clansmen and the settlers were probably oppressed by
food-rents which they could scarcely pay, and were
threatened with loss of land. Naturally they longed
for some body of written law, for freedom and equality,
and they were usually aided in the struggle by discon-
tented members of the chief houses.

The order of these conflicts, out of which the State
was built up in its ultimate form, must have varied in
different places, but on the whole tended to some such
course as this. The earliest form of fixed government
which Greek history shows us, the form which we find
in Homer, is that of heroic monarchy. This monarchy
is described by Aristotle as being hereditary and constitutional. No problem in early history is so difficult
to solve as that of the origin of kingship.[19] Among

---

[17] Maine, Early History of Institutions, p. 132. Immigrants on
Irish Tribe-Lands.
[18] Senchus Mor, iii. p. xxvi. Odyssey, xix. 109, 115, results of
εὐηγεσίη. .
[19] Pol. iii. 14. Cf. Kemble, Saxons in England, vol. i., and

most early peoples we find a certain stock or stocks, which are held almost divine. They differ so much from the common, that sometimes they are believed to have immortal souls, while their subjects lack them, or to transmigrate into nobler creatures after death. At the least they descend from Gods, as the English stock from Woden, or as Agamemnon from Zeus. Aristotle conjectures that the founders of the monarchies had been 'the first benefactors of the people in the arts of peace or war, or had first collected them into a society, or given them a territory to live in.' We only know that the kings of Homer's time are represented as possessing some strain of nobler blood than their free subjects, the chief of whom attend them in the council, and whom they consult in the greater assembly of the host. The kings are of the kin of Gods, διογενέες βασιλῆες, while most men are only δῖοι, or noble. It is not easy to understand the sort of nobility which was so general in the Homeric world. We are reminded of early Iceland, when 'nowhere was the common man so uncommon,' and of the fleet with which Cnut invaded England (1015), at least two hundred ships, and every man in every crew a noble-man.[20] Both kings and nobles were severed by an uncrossed line from 'churls rock-born or oak-born,' ἀπὸ δρυὸς ἢ ἀπὸ πέτρης, but either king or noble, if taken in war, might become a thrall.[21]

Freeman's Comparative Politics, Lecture IV. For the peculiarity of royal souls, Callaway's Religion of the Amazulu, ii. 197 : 'Chiefs turn into the black and green Imamba, common people into the Umthlcoazi.'

[20] Freeman's Norman Conquest, i. 373.

[21] Odyss. xix. 162; Preller, Ausgewählte Aufsätze, p. 179.

The heroic kingships, however they first arose, whether out of leadership in war or not, were usually hereditary, and hereditary rights were exercised over willing subjects, in accordance with traditional custom. The coronation oath was simply the laying hand on sceptre. The privileges of the king were a τέμενος far larger than the common lot, leadership in war, and probably many of the profits arising from fines, as well as the gifts which Hesiod says the kings used to devour, rewards for decisions in suits, and the chief seats at feasts, and the best mess at sacrifices. The heroic monarchy left to later Greece the institution of the General Assembly, and the germs of a council of elders, which might become probouleutic and administrative in an Oligarchy, or might be cut down to a mere committee, with the task of preparing matter for the consideration of the full Assembly, in a Democracy. (Pol. iv. 14, 14; vi. 8, 24. Gladstone, Homer, &c., iii. 58.)

'Kingship in a single city is not an institution which is likely to last;' for, as Aristotle says, many men would be found to be 'peers in valour and virtue,' and there is no mystery in a small community to protect the king. The members of the noble families would aim at equality, and some such anarchy would result as that which made confusion in the little isle of Ithaca before the return of Odysseus. Power would fall into the hands of all the noble houses in the clans, or into those of some one house, like the Penthelidæ in Mitylene, or the Bacchiadæ of Corinth, or the Protiadæ in Massilia, or the Basilidæ in Erythræ, who would cut down the royal functions, and hand over the real sway in commission to their own kindred. The kingly title might be left, but the man who bore it would only keep up the continuity of religious tradition, by performing certain rites and sacrifices. An instance of such a process has been noted among primitive peoples, our own contemporaries. Among the natives of Tonga the real ruling monarch yields precedence to a functionary whose duties are purely priestly, though his title means *King of Tonga*,[22] and whose position answers to that of Archon Basileus at Athens.

The new form of government by a clan, or by members of noble houses, when corrupted, is called a δυναστεία by Aristotle.[23] It corresponds to the worst sort of tyranny, or to the latest and most corrupt democracy, in the fact that old customary law was distorted to serve the selfish interests and passions of the rulers. Yet the δυναστεία claimed the noble name of 'Aristocracy,' the rule of the Best. The ruling class called themselves 'the good and fair,' 'the famous,' 'the illustrious.' They relied on long possession, on illustrious descent, on knowledge of the law, which was hidden from the *sheepskin wearers, dusty feet, club-carriers* of the country, and, above all, on possession of cavalry, which enabled them to ride down the dusty-feet as easily as the chivalry of feudalism used to crush the villeins.[24] Many causes contributed to the overthrow of the δυναστεία, or early oligarchy of ancient Greece. Trade increased, the seafaring popu-

---

[22] Sir John Lubbock, Origin of Civilisation, p. 347.
[23] Pol. v. 3, 3 ; Pol. iv. 5, 1.
[24] Müller, Dorians. Nicknames of Serfs, ii. 57.

lation grew strong and rich, the strength of light
infantry began to be understood, the poorer landholders were oppressed with taxes and usury beyond
endurance, the Oligarchy conferred honours and power
within ever narrower limits, and the general discontent
took the form of a demand for a written code of laws.
'When laws are written down, the rich man and the
weakling find equal justice,' says Euripides. This was
ordinarily secured after a struggle in which some neg-
lected member of the higher class was frequently the
leader. The lower classes, 'who have neither law nor
equity,' as a poet of the aristocratic class wrote, succeeded in making their leader æsymnete, as Pittacus
was in Mitylene, and looked to him as an irresponsible
magistrate to settle their differences with the nobles,
in a strife which went on till it was settled by the
giving of a code of laws, or, more frequently, silenced
by the rise of a *tyrant*.

V.

TYRANNIES IN GREECE.

THESE tyrannies, whether in Athens, under the Pisis-
tratidæ, in Megara, in Corinth, or elsewhere, helped to
consolidate and shape into their ultimate form the city-
states of Greece. All classes, noble or non-noble, were
crushed under the same weight of reckless power. All
were offended by the licence, so distasteful to Greek
ideas, which was permitted to women and to slaves;
and the pride of the nobles was sometimes humbled by

such insults as Clisthenes, tyrant of Sicyon, heaped on the tribes, calling them 'Ass-tribe,' 'Pig-clan,' and so forth. The tyranny may best be considered as the direct contradiction of all Greek ideas of life and government, as the negation both of the old notion of aristocracy founded on birth, and of the new notions of the equal claim of all freeborn citizens. The tyrant rules over men who are his equals and betters, purely in his own selfish interest, and not in that of the governed.[25] Just as a true commonwealth, or Politeia, contained all the elements of the State mingled in due subordination, so tyranny mingled the worst qualities of the worst forms of government, selfishness beyond that of the narrowest oligarchy, license beyond that of the loosest democracy. The tyrant in early Greece was generally either a demagogue, or partisan of the people, who led them against the nobles, and seized the fruits of victory, or one of the surviving heroic kings, who strained his hereditary and constitutional powers,[26] or a magistrate who abused the sway he held for a long term of office, or an oligarch set in high place by his faction. His power was never stable till he secured a bodyguard, especially a bodyguard of strangers. Once supported by this Oriental institution, he showed all the distrust of an oligarchy, all their greed, and like an oligarchy stripped the democracy of their arms, while in the spirit of democracy he put down the nobles, and drove them into exile less honourable than that of ostracism. Such crimes were the natural consequence of absolute power, though we should be wrong in supposing that

[25] Pol. iv. 10, 4.   [26] Pol. v. 10.

Pittacus of Mitylene, or Phidon of Argos, or Pisis-
tratus even at Athens, were essentially criminals of this
class.   They had the excuse of Cæsarism, and were not
wanting in the redeeming features which the believers
in despotism are wont to flatter.   But the tendency of
tyranny was to develop a character of lawless lust and
cruelty, a character to which recondite evil became good,
a fantasy which found pleasure only in arbitrary violence
against nature and law, in exquisite varieties of sin and
inflicted pain.   This is the type of man which we find in
the medieval cities of Italy, and the Baglioni may mate
with the Penthelidæ, Ezzelin with Periander.   But
there were also commonplace practices of tyranny, the
mere natural result of greed and selfishness of a low sort,
which have had their likeness in our own time.   When
we read how the tyrant is a stirrer up of war, how he
fosters distrust between citizens, how he puts down all
public gatherings, how he has his police everywhere,
how he encourages the extravagance of women, how he
impoverishes the State with public works, how he
associates with the worst of men, how he sets class
against class, how he corrupts all classes, we think of
the author of the Crimean and the Mexican expeditions,
and of the *coup d'état*, the cause of great men's exile
and of low men's promotion, the patron of Hausmann,
the tyrant who ' did so much for France.'

When the tyrants had been expelled, for the most
part, by the action of individual revenge for insult, or
of combined rebellion, or by help of the conservative
power of Sparta, the Greek states emerged from the
struggle, each a tolerably compact body of citizens,

united by the wrongs which all had suffered, and by glory in the tyrannicide which had benefited all. If the tyrant had not always succeeded in 'lopping off the taller ears of corn,' at least he had levelled nobles and churls, gentiles and non-gentiles, by a common oppression of disgrace. The emancipated citizens were now heirs to the splendid public buildings, the roads, and acqueducts, on which the tyrannic policy had expended public money.[27] In the common feeling of relief the class privileges, which had been in abeyance, fell often into disuse. In Athens, where the development of democracy was, so to speak, normal, the laws of Solon had, even before the tyrant's time, made property, not birth, the qualification for rule, and even the poorest freemen had received just so much power as would suffice to satisfy them. How much that may have been it is not easy to ascertain. In one passage Aristotle represents some disputants as holding that he 'gave *all* a right to sit on the juries, wherefore some blame him, as if he had rather undone than 'stablished the State.' The opinion that he *did* establish the juries, which in time made the Demos all powerful, as well as the blame, was probably expressed by the censurers of Solon, for (in Pol. book iii. 11, 8), as well as in the passage already quoted (ii. 12, 3), Aristotle himself declares that Solon only gave the people the right to elect magistrates, and to bring them to trial after their term of office. Whatever may have been the exact amount of liberty and power conceded, it is tolerably certain that the power could not have been actually wielded by poor and industrious men before

[27] Pol. v. 11, 8.

Pericles began the custom of paying the jurors.[28] The
laws of Solon, which were to the Demos what the laws
of Edward were to the English after the Norman Conquest—another name for justice and freedom, had the
good fortune to please both the people and the later
philosophers. Plato looked back to them lovingly, as
to the institutions of a time when our 'Lady Reverence
was with us;' and perhaps it was not till the Solonian
constitution was restored in all its exclusiveness by
Antipater and by a foreign force (322 B.C.), that the
Athenians discovered how their later democracy had
outgrown its early limits.[29]

Solon had anchored the State, with the fixed power
of the Areopagus, which exercised a censorial sway,
based on old religious privilege. It was the business of
Clisthenes, coming after the interval of tyranny, to
complete the equalisation of ranks which the Pisis-
tratidæ had begun. For this purpose he introduced
into the tribes many stranger-residents, and even slaves,
made new tribes altogether, and separated the citizens
into the local divisions of *demes* for political purposes,
while the *cláns* tended to become a mere religious survival,[30] and mode of registering the legitimacy of citizens.
What with new guilds, new tribes, and the bringing
together of the many separate family-worships into few
and common shrines, everything was contrived so as to

[28] Grote, iii. 170.
[29] Plato, Laws, 698, 744. δεσπότις ἐνῆν τις αἰδώς. Grote, iv. 139.
[30] Pol. vi. 4, 18; where Aristotle says that the same sort of
reform was carried out in Cyrene. Herodotus, v. 69, says he made
ten tribes instead of four, but supposes him to have done so out of
contempt for the sons of Ion.

blend the State into a new συνοίκισις. Changes almost as important followed the victory of the 'mob of seamen' at Salamis. The Archonship became open to all free citizens by *Lot*, the sacred power of the Areopagus was checked by Pericles and Ephialtes, the jurors were paid for attendance in the courts, the tables of the law were brought down from the Acropolis to the Agora, and step by step the demagogues reduced the democracy to that last estate which Plato calls a critical *theatrocracy*, and Aristotle despises as perverted and unnatural. But if Athens incurred the censure of Aristotle because, through the influence of trade, her population grew heterogeneous, because by aid of success in war she became a tyrant city, ruling other states against their will; if her citizens pursued commerce till they came to make money even out of their intellectual powers; if there was no drill, no surveillance of private life; on the other hand, Athens may be looked on almost as an Ideal State at the time when she placed full power in the hands of him who 'excelled all the state in virtue,' who was 'as a God among Men,' Pericles the Olympian. [31]

In Athens the development of the State was most natural and normal, but of course there were many varieties of growth, and many cases of arrested development in Hellas. In mountainous districts of Arcadia the people in Aristotle's time lived as an ἔθνος, or tribe, in separate homesteads. Sparta, again, knew no age of tyrants, and suffered from στάσις, or civil strife,

---

[31] Pol. iii. 13, 13; Grote, iv. 215. ὁ σχινοκέφαλος Ζεὺς Περικλέης, so called by Cratinus.

only in very remote times. She preserved the semblance of kingly power, in the two kings, with their sacred and military functions.[32] In many states, as in Thebes and Corinth, Oligarchy was as successful almost as Democracy was in Athens, and, in spite of insurrections, gave the stamp to the character of the city. Other states, again, lived without . fixed character, either Oligarchic or Democratic, and changed with each revolution that brought back one party of exiles, and drove the Government to wander in search of foreign aid, or gave dominion to a tyrant. When Sparta and Athens had fairly consolidated their powers, and had consciously recognised their state-character as Liberal or Obstructive, they were always interfering with the politics of the smaller towns, and so preventing a normal development.[33] Still on the whole there did exist a normal and natural law of revolution which, subject to occasional variations, governed the internal affairs of the Greek States. Having sketched their historical career to the period of full growth, it becomes necessary to examine the many causes that inclined the balance in every direction, from the loosest democracy to the sternest oligarchy.

[32] Herod. vi. 56.   [33] Pol. iv. 11, 17 ; v. 7, 14.

VI.

INTERNAL CAUSES OF VARIOUS FORMS OF THE STATE.

ARISTOTLE has left us an elaborate theory of the causes
which produced not only Oligarchies, Democracies, and
Tyrannies, but also the various degrees and shades of
difference that distinguished one from another Oligarchy
or Democracy. All three forms of constitution are in
the first place to be considered as παρεκβάσεις, as institutions which have missed the rational order, founded
on the very nature of things, which governs the real
Monarchy, the true Aristocracy, the genuine Commonwealth. To fall short of this perfection, then, was the
common feature of all existing non-ideal governments;
but they fell short of it in various manners and degrees.
They varied in their character—that is in their organic
arrangements as to the distribution of power, as to the
sovereign, or strongest portion of the state in the last
resort. The *sovereign* (κύριον) is 'that which decides
in questions of war and peace, and of making or dis-
solving alliances, and about laws, and capital punish-
ment, and exile, and fines, and audits of accounts, and
examinations of administrators after their term of
office.'[34] Clearly the character of the πολίτευμα or
constitution may vary almost infinitely—(and to observe the variety of shades was Aristotle's main pre-
occupation)—in proportion as few citizens or many
belong to the sovereign body, and in proportion to the

[34] Pol. iv. 14, 3.

degrees in which they share, and the manner in which they exercise sovereign functions, and the amount of discretion and power they allow to the elected magistrate. Judicial, administrative, elective, legislative functions may be arranged, in states so small as the Greek cities, in hundreds of artificial ways, so as to preserve a balance of power for a year or two.

States were thus differentiated as regarded the form of their constitution, and again they were differentiated by their moral object, by the kind of life at which they aimed. This aim, whether in Tyranny, Oligarchy, or Democracy, was a selfish one, namely the interest of one lawless ruler, of the few who were in power, or of the poorer freemen. All oligarchies, however, were not equally selfish and equally narrow, nor all democracies on one level of indolence, useless meddlesomeness, and greed. None of the perverted constitutions were *natural*, but none, not even Tyranny, might not be rendered more serviceable than total anarchy or constant change, by the moderate exercise of power which preserves the duration of governments, while duration might make even an oligarchy lose its virulence, as diseases grow milder when they have long prevailed in a country. This is the tolerant way in which Aristotle regarded all existing polities, however distasteful they might be to his own sense of right.

The constitution and character of a state depended on, and was in fact identical with, the distribution of power, and power was distributed in accordance with the proportionate differences in the social elements. There were rich men, poor men, men of middle fortune,

men who could afford heavy armour, others who went
light-armed to battle, and the bulk of the people derived its livelihood from trade, agriculture, or fishing
and maritime enterprise. All these classes of the
population, which might be reckoned in six sets, as
husbandmen, handicraftsmen, warriors, men of property,
priests, judges, had their various tasks, and claims to
power and recompense from the state, and the character
of the state was determined by the proportions in which
each class got its claims recognised. When men of
wealth and birth were powerful, they would exclude
husbandmen, handicraftsmen, and tradesmen from rule
—if possible even from the general assembly—on the
pretext that persons engaged in business had neither the
leisure necessary for the discharge of civil duties, nor
strength and skill in war. Where, on the other hand,
circumstances such as the victory of the seafaring population of Athens at Salamis, or a defeat in war which
weakened the aristocracy, threw power into the hands
of the multitude, they would establish Democracy, glory
in that as the only really free constitution, and reply
with the watchwords of ' equality,' ' rule and be ruled
in turn,' ' trust the sacred lot,' ' collective wisdom,' to
the Oligarch's pretension of wealth, education, and high
birth.[35] The constitution now established might vary,
Aristotle thought, in four degrees, resulting from the
nature and occupation of the ruling people. In a
Democracy, where the majority of the citizens were
husbandmen, and had little leisure to spend in the
market place, or where the holders of magistracies

[35] As to the Lot, Plato, Laws, 690 C.

were selected out of the possessors of a slight census, or even where all citizens were eligible for office, but the mass, being poor, had to attend to their own affairs, Law was likely to reign, and not popular self-will. But when there was a large population, paid out of the state resources, out of tributes, fines, and so on, for attendance at the Assembly, Law Courts, and Theatres, the last and worst form of Democracy arose. All the social evils of tyranny were felt; the people had its flatterers, as tyrants had theirs; justice was perverted by greed of fines. In such a state popular will ruled through decrees, instead of the passionless Νόμος, and the regulative powers of the upper house or πρόβουλοι were disregarded by the brawling Assembly.

When, on the other hand, birth, wealth, and education managed to make good their claims, when an Oligarchy was established, that too might be more or less intense in its action. A tolerably large class in easy circumstances might be the actual sovereign, or again, a very large property census might be demanded as qualification, or power might fall into the hands of one family or kinship, and, worst of all, the self-will of hereditary rulers might override Law. In contradistinction to these degrees of injustice, the Πολιτεία, or Commonwealth, was a form of well-tempered state, which united the virtues and satisfied the claims of freedom, wealth, birth, and native genius or virtue. Any form of Oligarchy or Democracy, or the juster Commonwealth, might be gradually brought about by slow transfer of the balance of power, by raising or lowering the franchise, electing to magistracies by vote,

an oligarchic arrangement, by lot, as Democracy preferred, or by combining both systems. In the Law
Courts there might be many degrees of property qualification, conferring the right to sit on trials, and many
shades of power might be entrusted to the Senate, to
the Nomothetæ, and to the Assembly. In oligarchies
and democracies all these matters were in a state of
delicate equipoise, which might be upset at any mo-
ment, with consequences affecting the whole state.
' The smallest thing may be the occasion of a revolution
really involving the most important results,' says Aristotle, whose theory of revolutions is an expansion of
this text.

VII.

THEORY OF REVOLUTIONS.

REVOLUTIONS, and civil strife, were the permanent
dangers of the Greek City-state, and the great bar
to its usefulness as an instrument of education, and
as an environment of the perfect life. As the character
of the citizen shifted with that of the city, and as that was
always changing, there could be no stable character at
all. Therefore what the Greek political theorist wished
to secure, before all else, was a *permanent* constitution.
As a rule he made the error of thinking that this could
only be found in a *stationary* condition of society,
which he found more nearly attained by Sparta than
by any other State. A theory of Revolutions was
therefore a necessary part of political philosophy, and

in Aristotle's theory the difference between the methods of himself and of Plato is very clearly displayed. Plato's views are made difficult to us by the fact that he starts from an astrological scheme of numbers which rule the existence of his ideal city. During a certain necessary cycle of time there will be certain births of inferior citizens among the Guardians; hence a selfish love of wealth, and of individual distinction arises, and the ideal polity is corrupted into a likeness of the warlike Spartan commonwealth. In the decline to Oligarchy, to Democracy, and to Tyranny, it is always the passion of greed that is the corrupting power. Oligarchic magistrates engage in commerce—a' practice, as Aristotle says, forbidden in most real oligarchies—they impoverish young men of birth, and thus a class arises like the Mirabeaus and Catilines of French and Roman history. The step to Democracy is easy, as the poor despise the bloated oligarchs, and at last attack them, while the extreme license of Democracy tends to the opposite evil of Tyranny. To all this theory Aristotle opposes facts. A State does not usually change into the form next it, but into its opposite. Oligarchy, more often than Tyranny, succeeds Democracy. Plato has given no account of the end of Tyranny itself. Injustice, and offence to heaven, more frequently than greed, produce revolutions. Lastly, the Platonic theory neglects the very many shades of difference which in real life separate democracy from democracy, and oligarchy from oligarchy. In the 'Laws,' however (709), Plato hints at a wider theory, and a more historical one.

In his own theory Aristotle is guided by history. The

' fountain' of Revolution was that jealous love of equality
which marked the Greek character. 'Men turn to civil
strife when they think that they have not got their dues
in proportion to their estimate of themselves,' Aristotle
observes.[36] The civil strife might take the form of a
desire to overthrow the existing constitution, or to seize
its rewards and offices, or to modify the intensity of its
character as oligarchic or democratic, or to change
some special detail in its working. On the whole a
Democracy was less subject to στάσις than an Oligarchy,
because there was room for the jealousy of 'an oligarchy
within an oligarchy,' and so for a tripartite division of
envyings and heartburnings. The universal and prevailing cause of Revolution was jealousy, but jealousy
had many objects, and took many shapes, and found
great variety of occasions. The distribution of wealth
and civic honours and office was of course the main
ground of quarrel, but habits of insolence, moments of
terror, the pride and negligence of overweening power,
the strength of some magistracy or class which had
outgrown its proper status (αὔξησις παρὰ τὸ ἀνάλογον),
the factiousness of party, the undue depression of any
set of citizens, were all predisposing causes of Revolution. Again, a State might contain citizens of alien
races, as Achæans and Trœzenians were mingled at
Sybaris, or as the Gephyræans were blended with an
Ionic population at Athens, and race hatreds might
break out into civil war. Even differences of local
situation afforded very pretty quarrels, and the dwellers
on the height might hate the dwellers in the plain;

[36] Pol. v. 1.

the people of the harbour might be more democratic than the people of the city.[37] 'In short, the acquisition of power, whether by private citizens, or magistracies, or tribes, or by any single portion, small or great, of the State, was a cause of sedition; for either the persons who envied these began the strife, or the men, or party which had gained the strength, were no longer content to live on a footing of equality with their fellow-citizens.'

Such were the general conditions of civil discord in Greece, but there were evils and dangers peculiar to Democracies, and others which beset Oligarchies. In a Democracy there was the terror felt by the rich, and their reactionary revolution against the peril of confiscation. The greed of demagogues would drive forth large troops of hostile *émigrés*, who waited their chance to destroy the Democracy. Then there was the risk, greater in warlike than in later times, of a demagogic dictator setting up a Tyranny. Any powerful magistracy might be made a stepping-stone to a despotism by an unscrupulous demagogue. Again, the proverbial haste of democracy which gave the force of law to suddenly carried decrees, might destroy some old legal safeguard of the constitution. In Oligarchies the besetting sin was insolence and injustice towards the mass of the citizens. Through this fault most of the old dynasties fell, under the assault of some popular leader, whether sprung from the oligarchic families, or of the oppressed classes. Allied to these dangers was the risk of narrowing the Oligarchy, and of constructing an

[37] Pol. v. 3, 15.

imperium in imperio. The insolence of wealth, and
the demands of luxury threw men of the type of Cati-
line or of Mirabeau, youths of ruined fortunes, on
projects of sedition. Distrust of the people in war
made mercenaries a necessity, and a general of mercenaries might anticipate the conduct of Italians like
Francesco Sforza and Castruccio Castrucani, and en-
slave the state he had served. Either in an Oligarchy
or a Democracy a change in the value of money might
widen or narrow the census, and a crowd of new
citizens might be admitted to power, or, again, office
might thus be limited to the few, and in either case
a revolution was imminent. As might be expected,
revolutions broke out on slight occasions, though really
the matters in dispute were of high importance. A
love quarrel, a lawsuit, a marriage difficulty, might
divide a city into parties, as in medieval Italy. The
words of Hallam apply almost without change to the
earlier civilisation of Greece: ' In every city the
quarrels of private families became the foundation of
general schism, sedition, and proscription.' In short,
the condition of Greek cities went to prove that ' the
pathological state is more frequent and more dangerous
in proportion to the complicated character of the
organism.'

In all these combinations of power, the form of the
constitution was the prize of party victory. This
state of things was positively ruinous to the philosophic
conception of the State. There could be no fixed
moral habit of character among men whose polity was
always shifting its ἦθος. To bring out the darkness of

the political picture, Aristotle sketches a brighter design
of the best possible State. He will not speak of the ideal
Aristocracy, where a few men, of preeminent merit, rule
the State for the advantage of the governed, nor of the
ideal Monarchy, where one divinely gifted man reigns in
the same fashion. Aristocracies demand somewhat beyond the real condition of States, or they approach the
form of government called Politeia. This is almost a
confession that the true Aristocracy, based on willing
concessions to half-divine superiority, is usually a mere
dream. A set of men, or one man, might flatter themselves, or their friends might flatter them, into the
belief that they were the founders of a true Aristocracy,
or of a true Monarchy. But in the eyes of Greece the
self-styled Aristocrats were really Oligarchs, and Aristotle himself did not escape the charge of being the
trencherman and boon companion of that slave-eunuch
turned tyrant, Hermeias. The philosophers might
expect much from an 'orderly tyrant,' 'young, temperate, quick at learning, having a good memory, of
a noble nature, and the friend and contemporary of a
great legislator.'[38] But the constitution of things was
against this favourable conjuncture of absolute power,
virtue, and knowledge. Monarchy of the true sort,
Aristocracy of the true sort, were but visions. 'There
are no kingships now,' says Aristotle.[39] There remains
the other natural and unperverted ideal government, the
Politeia, Polity, or Constitutional Commonwealth.

What was the Politeia? We have seen that Oligarchies and Democracies derived their names from the

---

[38] Plato, Laws, 709 E.   [39] Pol. v. 10, 37.

abnormal disproportionate growth of a part of their
organisation, from the monstrous development of the
power of poor or of rich. The more excessive the
deformity, the easier it was to give its name to the
deformed organisation, whether Oligarchy or Democracy. Now the Politeia has no distinctive name; it
is simply a constitution *par excellence*.[40] This fact in
style points to the distinctive merit of the Politeia in
nature. It had *no* overgrown part, all were mingled
in due proportion. The life of the Politeia, and of the
citizen in the Politeia, is established on the basis of
the μέσον, the golden mean. Property is equalised as
far as possible, extreme wealth and extreme poverty are
unknown. τῶν εὐτυχημάτων ἡ κτῆσις ἡ μέση βελτίστη
πάντων. Children are not brought up in the insolence
of luxury which 'breeds the Tyrant;' there is no
hiérarchie des méprises, as a modern philosopher has
nicknamed modern society. The natural tendency of
the City-state, the impulse of its being is allowed free
scope, for 'the city would fain consist of equals.' There is
a preponderant middle class, and rich and poor but little
exceed or fall short of the ordinary standard of wealth.
The full-armed   citizens hold the sovereign power.

---

[40] Compare Plato, Laws, 712. The fragments of Hippodamus, if
they are genuine, prove that these ideas of the value of mixed Governments were 'in the air.' εἰ καὶ σύνθετος ἀ πολιτεία ἤ καὶ συντεταγμένη
ἐκ πασᾶν τᾶν ἄλλαν. λέγω δὲ οὐ τῶν παρὰ φύσιν, ἀλλὰ κατὰ φύσιν·
τυραννίδος γὰρ οὐδεμία χρεία ταῖς πόλεσιν, εἰ μήπω καὶ τὰς ὀλιγαρχίας ἐπὶ
βραχύ. δεῖ τοίνυν βασιλείαν πράταν ἐντετάχθαι καὶ δεύτερον ἀριστοκρα-
τίαν. βασιλεία μὲν γὰρ θεομίματον πρᾶγμα, καὶ δυσφύλακτον ὑπὸ ἀνθρω-
πίνας ψυχᾶς· ταχέως γὰρ ὑπὸ τρυφᾶς καὶ ὕβριος ἀλλάσσεται. He goes on
to speak of the jealousies within oligarchies, and of the right the free
citizen has to γέρας from his State. Archytas is represented as saying,
δεῖ τὰν πόλιν ἐκ πασᾶν σύνθετον εἶναι τᾶν ἄλλαν πολιτείαν. Fuhr's
Dicæarchus, pp. 37, 38.

This State is clearly the best of possible constitutions, because it has the note of excellence, it is alone unshaken and unchanged by civil brawls. This is a picture of happy political life, as the philosophers hoped that it might be constituted. But when we ask where an example of the πολιτεία, of the 'well-mingled State,' is to be found, the answer is but doubtful. Sparta, perhaps, came near it, for the Spartan constitution held democratic, monarchic, and oligarchic elements in steady equilibrium. But Aristotle confesses—ἡ μηδέποτε τὴν μέσην γίνεσθαι πολιτείαν, ἢ ὀλιγάκις καὶ παρ' ὀλίγοις.[41] Thus he is at one with Tacitus, where he says—' delecta ex his et consociata Reipublicæ forma laudari facilius quam evenire,' though he would deny that, when the mixed State was once formed, ' haud diuturna esse potest.'

We have sketched Aristotle's analysis of the factors, historical, political, and social, that made up the Greek States, and the causes that disturbed them. The international relations of the States to each other must now be considered.

VIII.

INTERNATIONAL RELATIONS OF THE GREEK CITIES.

THE very essence of the Greek City-state was isolated, self-governed freedom. For a city to be subject to the

---

[41] Pol. iv. 11, 19. Solon also had the praise of 'mixing the State well,' as the Areopagus represented oligarchy; the elective nature of the governors, aristocracy; and the juries, democracy. (Pol. ii. 9.)

commands of another state in the regulation of her foreign affairs, was almost to cease to be a city at all, and to become a nondescript community, as much wanting in definite position as the once free citizen who has become the subject of a tyrant. Autonomy was as much the note of the free State, as a share in deliberative and judicial functions was the note of the full citizen.[42] Many reasons might be given to help to explain this peculiarly Greek demand of autonomous independence for each state, which caused at once the variety, the many-sided development, and the weakness and disunion of the race. The physical structure of Hellas, with its various climates, its deeply indented coasts, its walls of mountains, its different classes of productive soil, tended to sever city from city, and the mode of life in one state from the mode of life in another. To these natural causes must be added the force of religion, which combined the associations of ancestral kindred with those of locality. When once the religions of the *gentes* had been united under the sanction of a higher and more comprehensive worship, when once the city had been placed under the protection of an Olympic God, as Apollo, Athene, Hera, the limits of early Greek religion had been reached. The citizen, whose patron was Athenè, could not allow his state to be swayed by the citizens who worshipped Hera in chief place. 'The Gods are hard to reconcile,' and all the instincts of the Greeks prevented them from making the effort. True, it was religion that tried to unite city with city, just as religion had united γένος with γένος. The Amphic-

42 Pol. iv. 4, 11. αὐτάρκης γὰρ ἡ πόλις, τὸ δὲ δοῦλον οὐκ αὐταρκες.

tyonies of Calauria, of Delphi and Pylæ, the gatherings
at Delos and at Olympia, were all the result of a feeling
that tribes of Hellenes were one in blood and faith. It
might have been expected that, just as the old hospitali-
ties, in which one village received deputies from another
village to its sacred feast, had promoted the combination of villages into the city, so the meetings of Ionians,
Dorians, Dolopes, Perrhæbians, and so on, at Delphi and
Pylæ, would help to amalgamate cities into a nation,
or at least into a confederacy. But the greater Am-
phictyony was after all a survival from the tribal times,
from ages earlier, perhaps, than the foundation of the
City-states, which, when once founded, exercised so absorbing an influence over their citizens, that Greek states
never could coalesce into a Greek nation. Confederacies
there were in plenty, such as the Theban confederacy,
the Athenian alliance. But just as few Greeks, with
all their hatred of tyranny, could resist the temptation
of an opportunity to become tyrants, so neither Thebes
nor Athens could bear to be only first among equals. The
confederacies of the flourishing age of Greece were
always weakened by ambition on the one side and
jealous watchfulness on the other. There were, however, two causes which tended to promote a national
feeling in Greece, and to give a more than parochial
breadth to Greek politics, but these causes had ceased
to act in the age when Aristotle surveyed the constitutions of Hellas. Resistance to the barbarous power of
Persia in the struggle that saved civilisation went near
to combine all Hellenes, though, even in the face of
the Persian invasion, Thebes and Thessaly stood aloof,

Argos was doubtful, or took the side of barbarism. Again, after Persia ceased to be formidable, the strife for supremacy between Athens and Sparta divided Greece into two camps—the camp, in a sense, of Democracy, and the camp of Oligarchy, and it might have been hoped that the complete victory of either side would result in some sort of steadfast unity. But, unhappily, the pretext of liberty, whether urged by Athens or Sparta, only covered the ambition to erect a Tyrant State on the ruins of free Commonwealths, and the ultimate exhaustion of both powers left Greece, free indeed, but without a policy or an aim, save the sentimental policy of Isocrates, without even a wholesome dissension. When Thebes had grown to an equality with the two 'primary States'—Thebes, which in the struggle for the very existence of Greece had sided with the powers of darkness—a sound national feeling had ceased to be possible, and Greek politics became a chaos of petty and hostile ambitions. The new Athenian naval confederacy broke up disastrously; the backward States, Phocis and Arcadia, arose in sudden strength that had none of the polish of the old leading cities. The ambition of Phocis ended in the sack of Delphi, and in the consequent destruction of the associations that made the religious unity of Greece. Meanwhile the power of Macedon was growing up in the background, as surely and stealthily as the power of Brandenburg in modern Europe. The character of the individual Greek citizen had also been changing, his ideas becoming blurred and confused, through circumstances which need to be glanced at.

IX.

CAUSES AFFECTING THE PERSONAL CHARACTER OF THE
CITIZENS.

THE sources of dissension within the cities, and the causes of revolution which we have been considering, were all, it may be said, of a necessary character. It was necessary, if the States were ever to exist at all, that interests should clash, that there should be a struggle for power between sacred privilege and numbers, between wealth and birth, and the force of the majority and the might of individual ambition and genius. But when the struggle had been decided in one way or another, when the balance had been struck, which might unfortunately be so easily disarranged by a slight accéss of strength to the Demos, or to the Oligarchs, the cities had acquired each an individual *éthos*, or character. One was adventurous, industrious, full of variety of mood, yet constantly set on maintaining democratic freedom, like Athens ; one was steadily devoted to military glory, and submitted to military drill, like Sparta ; another was commercial, like Corinth ; another reposed indolently on the labour of an enslaved agricultural class, like Thebes. Whatever the *éthos* of the State, it was most important, for the avoidance of revolution, that the *éthos* should be impressed on all the citizens, and that the social tone should not be offended by individual vagaries, by ' a want of conformity to the standard of opinion in daily life,' like that which was censured in

Alcibiades. Besides the *éthos* of each state, there was what may be called the Hellenic *éthos*, the conformity to Greek ideas, to vary from which was to cease to be a good Greek, as to vary from the character of the State was to cease to be a good citizen. Now the character which the opinion of Hellas demanded from every true citizen might be summed in one word— Patriotism. Patriotism set the claims of the city above all other claims, urged the Greek to spend and be spent 'as if his body were not his own but another's,' in the interests of the State. The patriotism might be narrow, but it was genuine, and after the Persian war it was sapped by many causes. First came acquaintance with foreign lands, alien religions, non-Hellenic customs in daily life. Persian luxury and despotism, Oriental mysticism, and the wild rites of orgiastic religions, probably shocked the Greek at first; then they appealed to his love of power and his sensuality, then they set him to ask why the free institutions and temperate life of his country should be the best life. They were handed down to him by his ancestors, it is true, but wherefore should his ancestors be held wise with more than the wisdom of the Egyptians? These ideas led to speculation on the origin of society, *on its religious basis*, on the sanction of social rules, and in this era of enlightenment speculators were found, like the Thrasymachus of Plato, to denounce the life of the free State, to demand a return to Nature, and to defend tyranny. Political speculation was now set free, and metaphysical philosophy became more and more popular. Was it not a better and nobler thing, the Greek

had to ask himself, to strain all the mental faculties to
the apprehension of truth, and in the search after God,
than to haunt the Assembly, and mix in 'the Babel of
sterile politics?' Thus philosophy began to draw the
best minds away from the service of the State, into an
exclusive sect, while the ambitious were tempted, by
the sight of foreign luxury, to reject the old Greek
temperance, to desire unlimited wealth, splendour, and
power. Clubs and *Symmories* began to claim the attachment once felt for the γένος and for the city. Upon
luxury and culture followed indolence, and life became
too sweet to be wasted in the service of the State. Thus
mercenary forces began to be employed, and if any Greek
felt the old warlike impulse, he preferred to take arms
as a condottiere in Oriental or other service, where
booty was plentiful, rather than to stay at home and
defend the frontiers of his city.[43] Thus the younger
and poorer men were withdrawn from their states,
and this, with the increased luxury of the rich, and
with the fact that the old lots of land which supported a yeoman's family, were united in the hands of
a few great proprietors, along with the system of marrying 'in and in,' brought about that ὀλιγανθρωπία,
decline of population, which was the bane of Sparta.
On the other hand, there arose just the opposite evil,
as Aristotle thought it, for the commercial activity of
the maritime cities increased their population out of
measure; the spirit of colonising was spent; citizenship was too easily conferred, or might be claimed

[43] Plato, Laws, 701 C. On the 'Titanic' character of the later Greeks.

E

with less chance of detection. Thus the crowd of paid jurors, a pauperised aristocracy of thousands, was tempted to raise the never gratified cry of γῆς ἀναδασμός, to demand the meting out afresh of the lands of the rich, and did, if Aristotle is to be believed, inflict heavy and unjust fines, which went into the common fund for pleasures.[44] But the philosophers probably exaggerated the real proportions of the Red Terror in Greek democracies.

X.

PRACTICAL AIMS OF ARISTOTLE.

THE picture of the political state of Greece in the time of Aristotle, which has been sketched, is, perhaps, too darkly coloured. There was plenty of life left in Hellas, and she had not even yet 'completed her practical tasks in the domain of Politics.' But, on the whole, the spirit of her people was, for the future, to 'continue its activity in freedom from local boundaries,' was to flood the world with the light of civilisation, not to kindle a bright and solitary fire before the shrines of Apollo and Athene. To us, in the perspective of time, the unbroken continuity of Greek life is apparent, but to the contemporaries of Aristotle the new years seemed so different

[44] Confiscations by Demagogues, Pol. v. 5, 5. While the old Greek ideas prevailed, there would seem no injustice to the heirs in confiscation. The whole house had sinned with the sinner. Cf. Boeckh, Public Economy of Athens, Engl. Transl. 393. Does Dicæarchus say it was a favourite practice with the *Athenians* 'to entrap the resident aliens,' or is he speaking of the baser sort whom he calls the *Attici*, p. 141 ?

from the old, that they may well have thought the continuity stopped, the existence of Hellas ended. Greece was not dead, but changed—so changed that those who looked back to the years in which she best fulfilled her own ideas, the years of Salamis and Himera, when she withstood in one day the whole force of two alien barbarisms—or to the age of Pericles—might well have thought her dead. Yet we find Aristotle studying her political conditions, as if she were still the Hellas of times past, and we may well ask what was the nature of his practical hopes and aims.

In the first place Aristotle had to recognise the fact that, what with the weakening of Sparta and Athens, the rise of Macedon, the failing strength of the old natural enemy, Persia, what with the new cosmopolitan philosophies and the spread of enlightenment, national feeling, attachment to the city, exclusive pride in Hellenism, were waning forces. It has been suggested that he wished to revive the national sentiment, in the spirited words which contrast Greeks with the warlike and unsettled tribes of the North, and with the tame, though crafty Asiatics. ‘Greece might rule the world, if she came under one single government,’ he says, and the hint may imply a whole theory of an united Greece, combined with and absorbing the military order and drill of Macedon.[45] There is no word, however, to tell how Aristotle would have produced the union; whether it would have been a παμβασιλεία, a monarchy of the

---

[45] Pol. vii. 7. This is the view of Oncken, ‘Die Staatslehre des Aristot.’ ii. 272, 274 : ‘ Und bleibt als Panhellenisches Ideal des Aristoteles nur übrig, der Bund der Hellenischen Freistaaten unter der Schirmherrschaft des Makedonischen Königthums, &c.’

one best man, or a federation. But Greece would have
thought such a federation, under the leadership of
Macedon, as low as the subjection of Thessaly seemed
to Demosthenes, μὴ μόνον κατὰ πόλεις ἀλλὰ καὶ κατὰ
ἔθνη δουλεύειν. So slight is Aristotle's allusion, that we
are compelled to guess that he only glanced at the idea,
and put it away as one too happy ever to be realised.
If he did not hope then for an united Hellas, what
manner of political life did he still think possible for
Greeks, under the old political forms of the City-state?
To answer this we must remind ourselves of the extent
to which politics and morals blended and merged in
the minds of Greeks. The State was, as has often been
said, like an University, or, again, like a Religious
Order ; its drill, the devotion it claimed, were like the
enthusiasm demanded from his followers by the founder
of the Company of Jesus. Now if Greeks could either
forget that the sceptre of the world had passed from
Hellas, or could accept the old city life on a lower level
of dignity in face of the rest of the world, the old city
form might still suffice for the politico-moral training
of men. Aristotle, therefore, seriously studied all the
conditions of past Greek political experience, and, if he
could not cure the evils which vitiated the life of the
State, could at least put his finger on them, and say,
' Thou ailest here, and here.'

This kind of pathological examination of the states
and their disorders is, in short, Aristotle's *practical*
contribution to Greek State-lore. His minute diagnosis
of the diseases of the polities had never been so well
attempted before, and, as he himself said, if we know

the causes of the ruin of states, we know the remedies. In the first place even the most minute violations of Law were to be scrupulously guarded against, for the accumulative force of many small changes destroys the strength of Law, which lies in Custom. Here Aristotle is far enough removed from our conception of Law as a living thing, that developes with the changes of society, and he rather holds to the ancient theory which wished to stereotype and fix society in a stationary condition. Again, the party of the State which possessed power should never use it to harm ' those within or those outside of the constitution.' Thus he recommends short terms of rule, as short as six months, to avoid all appearance of injustice in a State where many share the highest franchise. Short terms of office, also, are unfavourable to the growth of tyranny. Again, in oligarchies and polities, where there is a money qualification for the highest franchise, there must be a yearly census to prevent a depreciation, or a rise in the value of money, from disturbing the balance of the State. And this is only one practical way of guarding against the disproportionate growths of power, which destroy the artistic symmetry and pervert the very life of cities. A censorship should watch over private morals in the same interest, and rich and poor should be made to feel that they are not hostile camps, but have the same real interests in political permanency. This will follow from a system of unpaid magistracies, which the poor will desire less, and whose holders they will not envy.

In Democracies, not only should all clamours for division of property be repressed, but not even the incomes of the rich should be subject to disproportionate charges. Aristotle disapproves of the large and unnecessary expenses incurred by volunteers at Athens, to provide spectacles, banquets, and music for the enjoyment of the Demos, though one might suppose that, where there was no wasteful extravagance, such liberality was a happy mode of keeping up φιλία between rich and poor. To be brief, Aristotle advises all governments, of whatever shade, to avoid being too emphatically themselves. The less democratic a demos is, the less oligarchic an oligarchy, the less tyrannous a tyrant, the more each of these forms of rule approaches the natural 'mean,' and the more likely is it to last undisturbed.

Practically, then, Aristotle recognises the State, even in its erring forms, as a most valuable educational organism, whose value improves with its permanency. It might, even in his late time, remain the best environment of the noble life. And thus Aristotle did not think it below him to frame laws for his native city of Stagira, where, even in the fourteenth century of our era, he was revered 'as thoughe he were a seynte,' and where men hoped 'that through inspiracioun of God and of hym, they schulde have the better Conseile.'[46]

[46] Mandeville, Voyage and Travaile, p. 16.

XI.

SLAVERY, COMMERCE, AND THE LATER DEMOCRACIES.

THE mind of Aristotle, like the Greek State system itself, was influenced by traditional ideas older than the development of the State, and he attempted to apply these ideas at a period of history when the State was being sapped and weakened by many novel forces. The confused result is very plain in Aristotle's discussion of the questions of Slavery, of Commerce, and of ultimate Democracy. In the first place he was anxious to support the Conservative view of the institution of Slavery. This view was threatened on many sides. In the sphere of politics, both Tyranny and Democracy tended to relax the restraints imposed on slaves, and we learn from Xenophon, as well as guess from Aristotle, that the slaves in Athens were well-to-do, richer than many citizens, free and easy, not distinguishable in their attire by the one-sleeved tunic, not to be struck by men who were not their masters. Again, the new theories were all against slavery. Speculators called it a violation of Nature, just as Rousseau did so many centuries later.[47] The Flesh and Blood argument of Mr. Gladstone was applied to slavery. 'God made all free, Nature has made no man a slave,' said Alcidamas. 'No one is worse when he becomes a slave, who was

---

[47] Rousseau, *Discours*, p. 65 :—' Se trouve-t-il un homme d'une force assez supérieure à la mienne, et de plus assez dépravé, assez paresseux, et assez féroce, pour me contraindre à pourvoir à sa subsistance pendant qu'il demeure oisif ; il faut qu'il se résolve à ne me pas perdre de vue un seul instant.'

good when a freeman,' said Euripides, contradicting
the Homeric saw,

ἥμισυ γὰρ τ' ἀρετῆς ἀποαίνυται εὐρύοπα Ζεὺς
'Ανέρος, εὖ τ' ἄν μιν κατὰ δούλιον ἦμαρ ἕλησιν.

Again, 'if one be a slave, he hath the same flesh as the
free, for no man ever was born a slave by Nature; but
evil fortune has enslaved his body.' [48]

In opposition to this sentiment, and in accordance
with his firm belief in old Greek ideas, Aristotle goes
to work to prove that slavery is natural. One argument
comes easily to hand; all Nature is arranged as a
hierarchy of rulers and ruled, and it is necessary to the
safety of society that the element of society which has
full reason should direct the element that has mere
bodily strength. The poets had said as much: 'It is
right that Hellenes should rule barbarians.' (Eurip. *Iph.
Aul.* 1400.) This text proves that the idea is an orthodox
one; besides, everything Nature makes has *some* purpose, nay, has *one* purpose, and to what purpose were
barbarians created except to be slaves, and wild beasts
except to be hunted? Again, a household is a *natural*
community, and to suffice the wants of this community
there must be instruments. Now instruments will not
work at the word of command, so there is absolute need
of *living* instruments. The poor man has only his ox,
but *Nature* (improving on this early state of the slave-
less Phocians) has provided slaves, that is, men who are
naturally not their own property.[49] Slaves differ as

---

[48] Cf. Oncken, 'Staatslehre des Aristoteles.' Vol. ii. p. 34.

[49] Athenæus, 6. 86, 88: 'Phocians had no slaves at one time. Slaves
may be divided into the classes of slaves bought, slaves bred in the

much from other men as body differs from soul, and beast from man. The best thing they have to contribute to the community is simply their bodily strength. Here we meet the difficulty that Nature has separated body and soul, man and beast, by obvious unmistakable differences. Now why has she not separated citizens and slaves as widely? To answer this Aristotle looks about for visible differences. First, slaves are barbarians; again, slaves have not the erect port which the freeman gained from the gymnasia and arms, forbidden to the unfree. Aristotle was unfortunate in the fact that the slaves of the Greeks were not negroes, for then he might have said in earnest, what Montesquieu said in irony, about the impossibility of supposing that God had meant to give freedom to beings with such ill-formed noses.

Aristotle's search for an universally acknowledged difference between the shape and semblance of slaves and freemen being half a failure, he has to declare that *Nature* '*wishes* to make their bodies different.' But *Nature*, as we have seen, does not always get her own way. It is for the philosophers to detect her intentions, and explain them, and therefore Aristotle proclaims that *Nature* has made the two classes of free and slave, though she has only occasionally succeeded in making the difference visible. ('Η δὲ φύσις βούλεται μὲν τοῦτο ποιεῖν πολλάκις, οὐ μέντοι δύναται.) (A later chapter sets out that the slave is indeed a man,) but that his virtues

family, and slaves taken in war. The Chians were the first buyers of slaves. There were slaves attached to sacred territory, and unfree land-serfs.' Cf. Hermann's 'Lehrbuch der Griechischen Antiquitäten,' iii. 79–90.

only correspond to those of the part of the soul which
is obedient to reason. To soften the severity of the
argument, Aristotle alleges that the relation is for the
good of the slave (accidentally), as well as (essentially)
for the good of the master. Moreover, there is an af-
fection of a sort between master and slave, and through
his relations to the master the slave is 'a partaker in
common life,' as indeed he is accepted into the religious
services of the household to which he belongs. He may
also, if he be a free-born Greek taken in war, console
himself by reflecting that he is not *naturally*, but only
casually, a slave.

In this argument Aristotle uses Nature in his
favourite sense of the perfected development of institutions. The State is such an institution.[50] The State
consists of freemen at leisure, and only through slave-
labour is that leisure to be obtained. The philosopher
has passed beyond even the old aristocratic sentiment
of Homer's time. Odysseus was a practised ship-builder
and husbandman; but Aristotle's burghers would disdain
to hew wood, and to dig they would be ashamed. Thus
slavery is necessary, and, like Plato in the Laws (777 D),
Aristotle would prefer to have barbarous slaves of various
speech, rather than to employ an earlier subject population of Greeks, as did the Thessalians and Spartans.
The theory seems odious to us, because we have been
used to see the old institution, which in ancient society
had a meaning and a purpose, namely the attainment of
the perfect life, existing in a society with a changed con-
science, and a changed purpose—money-making.

[50] Pol. i. 1.

To understand and to forgive Aristotle's opinions on slavery, let us remember what Christian philosophy of the best period had to say on this matter. Ægidius Romanus, a pupil of S. Thomas Aquinas, reasons thus: Man has fallen from the liberty he had in Paradise, has lost the right to belong to himself, and is thus *naturally* liable to be made a slave. Again, he is *legally* liable to become a slave, if he is taken captive in war. The author of the 'Summa Theologiæ' also avers that slavery though unnatural before the Fall, is now rather an addition to, than a departure from, the Law of Nature.[51]

When theology aids political speculation in this happy way, there is clearly a deep and powerful conviction of human nature at the bottom of the theory that slavery is natural. The cause of this conviction is long custom.[52] Captives taken in war pay with their liberty the ransom of their lives. Again, children are naturally the *property* of their parents, who, in Greece, might sell them till they reached the age of seven. Again, certain disgraceful actions have in most ages been punished with loss of liberty, and in early times men gambled away their bodies and their freedom, or bowed their necks for bread in time of famine, or lost their liberty through debt. Thus all nations have been familiar with the fact of slavery, and with the theory of naturally distinct classes of men. When philosophers, as culture advanced, have tried to discover the ideal, and the aim of life, they have looked on it as the aim of the best class, and have found a fitting function for

[51] Ad Franck, 'Réformateurs et Publicistes de l'Europe,' 89, 90. S. Thom. Aq. Prim. Sec. ix. xciv. 5.
[52] Kemble, 'Saxons in England.' The Unfree.

the other classes in mere service. All this is shocking
to us, who neither believe in natural distinctions of
classes, nor in any universal aim of life, except that of
' getting on 'in the world.' We therefore leave all
nominally free to strive towards this noble goal, which
we well know that only the few can reach. The ancients,
and the Christian doctors we have alluded to, were
equally well aware that but few could attain to their
very different goal—Perfection. The former accepted
slavery as a means towards that end, the latter knew
that no earthly condition made its attainment impossible.

Finally, we must remember that no one would have
been more bitter than Aristotle against the negro-
slavery on plantations of modern days. To turn the
servants of the noble life into tools of limitless money-
making, would have been, in his view, unnatural. We
must remember also, that he would have held up the
promise and reward of freedom, to stimulate his serfs
to virtuous lives, and, with freedom in prospect, and
friendship in the meantime, with every lovely rite of
divine service performed for their sake, there may have
been worse lives than those of the Greek slaves.[53] The
heroic fathers of their masters had often borne the yoke,
when captured in battle, and the father of the Ionian
race, Apollo, the mediator between men and Zeus, had
come down to earth upon a time, and had been the slave
of the king Admetus. Thus, while we may wish to see

[53] Œcon. I. vi.:—Δίκαιον γὰρ καὶ συμφέρον τὴν ἐλευθερίαν κεῖσθαι
ἆθλον· καὶ τὰς θυσίας καὶ τὰς ἀπολαύσεις μᾶλλον τῶν δούλων ἕνεκα ποι-
εῖσθαι, ἢ τῶν ἐλευθέρων, πλείονα γὰρ ἔχουσιν οὗτοι οὗπερ ἕνεκα τὰ
τοιαῦτα ἐνομίσθη.

a state of things in which life shall have a noble aim, towards which all shall be equally free to strive, we cannot agree with writers who allege that 'Plato and Aristotle, with almost cynical heedlessness, sacrificed the toiling multitude to a select moral oligarchy, who appropriated the virtues by a kind of natural selection.' If the domestic slave, the bright side of whose lot we have sketched, and if the husbandman slave in his subject commune, and his life under a Grecian sky, were 'cynically sacrificed,' what shall we say of our own miners, and of our own starved and ignorant peasantry?

Aristotle found that Nature was in conformity with Greek practice in the matter of Slavery. But Nature was out of conformity with Greek practice in the matter of Commerce. Aristotle proves this by using 'Nature' in the reverse of his usual way. Slavery was natural, because it was a finished result of the working of circumstance and reason in human life. Money is unnatural, because money is not a *primitive* institution, but the result of a covenant, that is, the result of the working of circumstance and reason in human life.

Acquisition of all things absolutely needful, beginning with food, which Nature provides for the chicken in the egg, is *necessary*, and thus barter is *natural*, as it provides things necessary, and no more. But money is neither a *natural* product, nor a thing of any intrinsic usefulness, nor a thing to the desire and collection of which there is any fixed *limit*, and, though dead matter, it manages in some unholy fashion to breed its like, in the shape of interest. Commerce employs this unnatural substance, and commerce makes gain from the

other party to the bargain, while usury is a sort of
crime, like 'sweating' the coin. In this tirade against
money Aristotle is really taking up a position like that
of Rousseau. He wants to go back to a state of nature
in which barter supplied all natural wants, and forgets
that, without money, no civilisation like that which he
delighted in, and no intercourse between polished nations, would have been practicable. He forgets, too,
that, even before money was invented, people might
find no *limit* to wealth-seeking. The ζωὴ ἄσπετος of
Odysseus (Od. xiv. 96) went beyond limit of his con-
sumption, and its aim was, not nurture, but power, as
he could make grants to his *comitatus* out of his herds
and flocks. (In fact Aristotle is carried away by the old
aristocratic hatred of trade, as marked in Greece as ever
it was in feudal Europe. He has the Socratic contempt
for any man who 'prostitutes' his courage for gain, as
a soldier, or his eloquence for gain, as an orator, or his
wisdom, as a teacher. All such conduct makes that an
instrument which should be an end.)The love of money
has brought strangers into all cities, and spoiled the
éthos, and confused the customs. Money has put power
in the hands of men of no birth, and has enabled the
Demos to leave his handicrafts or field-labour, and
attend to politics, and pay himself by confiscations.
For it is difficult for the poor to meet in unpaid Assemblies, and, where there are no revenues, this paying
of Assemblies is hostile to the few, for the money must
come from taxes, and fines, and unjust courts of Jurors.
(Pol. vi. 5, 5.)

If commerce had not been unduly developed, if

Athens had not been the mart of all the world, her
revenue from dues and customs would have been much
smaller; there would have been no great fortunes, and
liberal rich men; nothing, in fact, to tempt the people
to desert the country for the town. She would have con-
tinued to be the early democracy, or polity, of husbandmen, not the last democracy of craftsmen and hirelings.
Without spectacles, gratuitous distributions of food,
without the feasts and ceremonies, ' such as no other city
in Greece rejoiced in,' the poor would not have crowded
into Athens, would not have been half supported by the
State, and enabled to make their decrees law. Without
the intercourse of trade, they would not have spoken in
an accent, and worn garments, and practised customs,
' mixed up out of all that Greeks and Barbarians use
separately.'[54]   Commerce, in short, made the laxest
democracy possible, and the laxest democracy was as
fond of fining the rich, as fond of pleasure, as given up
to flatterers, as the tyrant.   It is easy to oppose facts
to these charges of Aristotle, as far as they are urged
against Athens; easy to allege that the heliastic oath
ensured the State against any selfish injustice of the
people, to show that the steady undebased standard
of coinage proves a rare political honesty; that the
Nomothetæ, and the trials for illegal proposals, must
have checked the popular will as expressed in decrees;
and it may even be asserted that the Theoric fund
answers to our Church endowments, instead of to the
civil list of a Tyrant. On the other hand, many of the

---

[54] Xen. Ath. Rep. iii. 1. and ii. 8.   Pol. vi. 4, 5.:—ἡ τελευταία
δημοκρατία.

religious feasts were ἐπίθετοι ἑορταί, innovations on the
old religion, and were pampered while the ancient rites
were stinted. The evidence of Isocrates, Xenophon, and
the Comedians is on the side of the philosophcal foes of
ultimate democracy.   The philosophers preferred to
look at the dark, the modern historians enjoy the
bright, side of the character of the great city, whose
very degeneracy was a not unlovely scene of common
enjoyment, of noble pleasures, and artistic luxury.
The enjoyment was too incessant, the art too luxu-
rious, the life too bright and variously blended to
last. ' The constitution of things proved somehow
to be against it;' but this was only half the reason
of the censure freely spoken by Plato, Aristotle,
and Xenophon. They echoed, in a stately way, the
grumbling of rich men, who, on the whole, were probably not ill-satisfied with their native city, which
declined because 'everything which has a beginning
has also an end,' and because even the city that was
"the Rose of Greece' had its term like other flowers.
(Lysippus ap. Dicæarch. p. 141.)

<hr />

XII.

ARISTOTLE'S IDEAL STATE.

THERE is nothing more characteristic in Greek political
feeling than the almost religious attachment to the
State. The Athenians of Pericles' time considered their
very lives not their own, but the possession of the City,

through which alone their lives were, in their eyes, free
and worth keeping.[55] We have already pointed out the
many causes that broke up this feeling of devotion, and
proofs of the change in sentiment may be found in
Aristotle's conception of the ideal State. It is true
that no one speaks out more clearly than he as to the
supreme position of the city, which is, as he puts it,
prior *in idea* to the family and the citizen. The family
and the individual only exist, he almost seems to hold, as
factors which are at last to compose that ultimate and
perfect whole, the State. Yet when we come to examine
his ideal State ($\kappa\alpha\tau'$ $\epsilon\dot{\upsilon}\chi\dot{\eta}\nu$), we cannot but detect traces of
a wish to make the State an organism to subserve the
happiness of the individual.[56] It is true that, in af-
fording an environment, and all outward appliances of
perfect happiness, as well as in supplying all the human
relations within which perfect virtue may be exercised,
the State also attains to what Aristotle thinks its own
proper perfection. But it cannot be concealed that
Aristotle's conception of perfect happiness is somewhat self-regarding. His citizens, no less than the
citizens of Plato, are all to be philosophers, and their
bliss is a philosophic satisfaction.) Now a State which
made this philosophic, nay almost mystic, ecstasy possible for all its citizens, would, in practice, have been
likely to slip out of the active inter-political life of
Hellas, and would have been prosperous only if it were
'possible that a state should be planted somewhere in

---

[55] Pol viii 1, 4   The same view empressed by Aristotle.
[56] Curtius' History of Greece, v. 205 (Engl. Transl.). 'The spiritual
life of the Individual became the standard whereby to judge of the
Commonwealth.'

isolation.' Thus, with all his caution, Aristotle, like
Plato, cannot reconcile himself to the natural and spon-
taneous ideas of Hellas.

There are one or two expressions in the ' Republic' of
Plato which strike a kind of key-note, prolonged with variations, in the 'Ideal State' of Aristotle. Plato writes:
' If Philosophy ever finds in the State that perfection
which she herself is, then it will be seen that she is in
truth divine ;' and again: 'The question is how the study
of philosophy may be so ordered as to be consistent with
the preservation of the State.'[57] Now Aristotle, too, con-
ceives ' an End ($\tau\acute{\epsilon}\lambda o s$) which shall be the same for the
perfect man and the perfect State,' a standard of virtue
which shall be the same for the individual and the State.[58]
This end is attained, and this standard reached, by those
only who possess ' the good things of the spirit that are
the more precious even as they are the more exceeding
abundant,' in contrast with outward wealth, which has
a natural limit. Such men, and a state composed of
such men, are alone to be called happy, nay *blessed*
with a bliss beyond all the mere good repute and praise
that is given to justice.[59] 'No man eulogises happiness
as men praise justice, but he calls it " blessed," as something better and more divine.' Again, in the same
passage of 'The Ethics,' he says: 'We hold the Gods to
be blessed and happy, and even so we call the most
divine of men blessed.' Compare the words in ' The
Ethics,' where the Deity is adduced as an example of
the blessed estate resulting from the full possession of
virtue and wisdom, and an existence in harmony with

[57] Rep. 497 C.		[58] Pol. vii. 15.		[59] Eth. i. 12, 4.

these. From these texts it follows that the ideal State of Aristotle, with its citizens who are called ' blessed' (μακάριοι), does not rest on mere political and moral virtue. Moral virtue is a thing not beyond the reach of praise, not too rare and holy for comparison with other conditions, and for encomium. The τέλος, the ultimate end of the happy life, is, by its very essence, unattainable in the merely righteous existence of the law-respecting citizen. It is like the happiness of the Gods (Ethics, x. 8, 7), who ' alone are all blessed, yet not through a life of moral practice. For what actions of morality can we assign to them—acts of justice? There is something ludicrous in the conception of their keeping covenants, and making exchanges— . . . . acts of generosity—to whom will they make gifts?'—and so on. Yet there is an activity of self-conscious life in the blessed beings, who do not sleep like Endymion, which can be nothing else than the ecstatic contemplation called θεωρία. Now (Eth. x. 8, 8) the life of mortals is only happy so far as it has a kind of likeness to this divine activity. ὥστ' εἴη ἂν εὐδαιμονία θεωρία τις.

From this conception of Happiness, apart from action, which is to be the portion of the perfect man in the perfect State, it follows that Aristotle, like Plato, wants to devise a State which may be preserved in full civic life, while at the same time it affords a *milieu* for the mystic life. In this polity the philosopher will not be a forlorn stranger, but will find the satisfaction of the civic and political sentiment of Greece, and also the enjoyable and satisfying *activity* of the divine part of

his nature; will, in fact, live *the best life of practice,
and the blessed life* too, in the society of his peers
(ὅμοιοι).[60] In such a city his happiness will not be subject to the reproach of do-nothingness, with which the
philosophers in the ordinary States of Greece were
justly assailed. How then are these peers in philosophy,
this company for the leading of the best life, to be
fitted with the χορηγία or necessary outward appliances
and goods of a free, temperate, generous existence?
How is their city to be ordered and governed?

These are the questions discussed in the 7th and
8th books of the 'Politics' of Aristotle. Keeping his aim
always before us, it is easy to understand the limitations
of his ideal State. It is neither to be a state organised
merely with a view to the fostering of martial valour—an
encampment, as it were, like Sparta—nor a commercial
city, eager for wealth, and making itself all men's mart,
like Athens. From the example of the Spartan discipline Aristotle borrows the idea that it is possible to
keep a city constant to an aim, possible to enforce simplicity of life, and uniformity of drill and of education.
From Plato he continues the idea of a city of philosophers, but, unlike Plato, he attempts to bring in no
innovation, to establish no institution, such as community in wives, children, and property, which experience
shows to be contrary to the universal instincts of humanity. Thus we may conceive of the ideal State of
Aristotle as almost Platonic in its aim, almost Spartan
in the strictness of its discipline, but always limited by

---

[60] Pol. vii. 2, 1; Pol. vii. 2; 5. καθ' ἣν τάξιν κἂν ὁστισοῦν ἄριστα
πράττοι καὶ ζῴη μακαρίως.

the thought of conditions which history proves to be
necessary, and widened by the desire of liberal enjoyment.

In the first place, then, the founder of a city of
men who are to be peers in their capacity for leading
the highest life, must be allowed to choose citizens of a
noble nature, men of spirit and intelligence. Again,
they must not be too numerous, as a large state is not
easily kept to its discipline, nor do the citizens find it
possible to gain the requisite knowledge of each other's
capacity for rule, while strangers slip unnoticed into
the roll of citizens.[61] States, too, have their natural
and necessary *limit*, like all other things, in art and
nature. The natural limit of a state is found in the
number of citizens necessary to provide the political
conditions of sufficiency (αὐταρκεία) in every respect.
The extent of land must be just so great as to support
this number of citizens and their families in a life of
freedom, leisure, and *temperance;* to feed their agricultural labourers, who are to be unfree; and to supply
provisions for the priesthoods and sacrifices of the Gods.
Thus the ὅμοιοι are all *landholders*, and so are *nobles*.
As nobles at leisure, they will be enabled to live the
higher life of excellence, on which their happiness de-
pends. Any form of labour, or of commerce, would
absorb the leisure absolutely necessary for the happy
and completely virtuous life. 'The citizens must not
live the life of traders, nor of artisans, for that existence
is ignoble, and opposed to virtue, nor must our citizens
be husbandmen, for there is absolute need of entire

[61] Scrutiny at Athens generally detected crowds of aliens.

'leisure for the development of virtue and for the conduct of political affairs.'

Men who provide, either as artisans, tradesfolk, or husbandmen, for the wants of the citizens, are, as being incapable, *ex hypothesi*, of the precise life, no *element* in the State (μόριον), but only *conditions* out of which the material structure of the State is built. The full citizens are, so far, in the position of the full citizens of Sparta, but their leisure is not given up to warlike training alone, but to culture. Their agricultural labourers are to be unlike the Helots, for they are to be, as far as possible, men who do not share the same blood and speech, nor are they to have the warlike valour of the Helots. The land is to be so divided that each citizen shall have two lots, one near the border of the State, like the properties called ἐσχατιαί in Attica, the other near the city. Thus the citizens will all be equal in their interests as well as in their training, and none of the demes will oppose a war because it ravages their estates, and leaves unharmed the lands of demes nearer the town. On private lands the slaves are to be private property ; on the folk-lands and temple-lands, public property. The many dangers which arise from inequality of property, from a χορηγία which is not σύμμετρος, are thus in part provided against. Landed property is equalised, and only from his land can the citizen who is true to the theory of *natural wealth* derive riches. Again, no citizen is exposed to the risk of losing his franchise through inability to provide for his own meal at the common tables. The subscription to these, by an improvement on the Spartan practice, is defrayed out of the produce of the folk-land.

Thus leisure is secured to all the citizens. There remains, however, a danger to equality of wealth, in the chances of making large fortunes by commerce. Thus the question is raised, shall the ideal State be near the sea?

Without sharing Plato's horror of the 'bitter, brackish element, filling the streets with merchants and shopkeepers, and begetting in the souls of men uncertain and unfaithful ways,' Aristotle yet keeps in mind his own doctrine that ' a naval power is ever democratic.' He is anxious to keep out strangers nurtured in alien laws, to check the overflowing population of a seaport, and yet to have the means of importing the necessaries of civilisation. His State is to be a mart for her own good, not for others' profit, and thus requires a harbour near the city, yet not too near. Again, he will have a navy, if his State is to be a leading State in Greece, but the ναυτικὸς ὄχλος shall no more share in the State than the husbandmen. The officers and fighting men on board ship alone are to be freemen, and of the ruling class. Aristotle can allow himself this license of fancy in a State κατ' εὐχὴν, and he finds an instance of the possibility of an unfree naval force in the case of Heraclea, in Pontus, where the Periœci manned the navy. Indeed, the oarsmen, even in Athens, must as a rule have been slaves : those who rowed at Arginusæ were rewarded with their freedom. The demand for slave seamen shows that Aristotle's ideal State is based, as much as Plato's, on the existence of supposed natural distinctions among classes of men Plato frankly proposes to get these distinctions generally admitted, by telling the ' noble lie' that there are gold, silver, and iron species

of men.   Aristotle backs his conception of exclusive divisions, proposed in Book I., by the historical instance of
Castes in Egypt.[62]   'Apparently it is not to-day, nor
even lately, that the discovery has been made by theorists
on constitutional government, that the State should be
marked out into castes (hereditary classes), and that the
element which fights should be separate from that
which tills the soil.   For this is the case even now in
Egypt, and also in Crete; Sesostris, it is said, having
legislated to this effect for Egypt, and Minos for Crete.'
In the same way Plato, in the 'Timæus,' makes the
Egyptian priest say to Solon, 'If you compare our laws
with your own, you will find that many of ours are the
counterpart of yours as they were in the olden time.
In the first place, there is the caste of priests, which is
separated from all the others; next there are the arti-
ficers, who exercise their several trades by themselves,
and without admixture of any other; and also there is
the class of shepherds, and that of hunters, as well as
that of husbandmen; and you will observe, too, that
the warriors in Egypt are separated from all the other
classes, and are commanded by the law only to engage
in war.' [63]   There seems very little reason to believe
that a rigid caste system ever existed in Greece, though
we hear of families among which certain crafts, and
music, and the performance of sacred rites were hereditary.   But the idea of *natural* distinctions among
men, distinctions which Nature did not quite succeed in
marking by physical differences, was congenial and useful

[62] Pol. vii. 10, 1–6 ; Herodot. ii. 164–167.
[63] Plato, Timæus, 24 A.

to both Aristotle and Plato, who, believing that events
return in cycles, might easily look forward to a revival
of a system of castes.

Aristotle has thus provided against most of the un-
toward wants that caused jealousies in Greek cities,
and disturbed the happy life with politics that threatened to subvert the city. He has, as far as possible,
equalised possessions, taken care that there shall be no
extremes of riches and poverty, has secured leisure for
all true citizens, excluded evil foreign influences, and now
he comes to the question of the sovereignty. Who is to
hold power? Clearly only the host, the men at arms.
'Those who have weapons in their hands have also in
their hands the permanence or non-permanence of the
Constitution.' This cannot include the democratic light-
armed troops ($\psi\iota\lambda\grave{\eta}$ $\delta\acute{\upsilon}\nu\alpha\mu\iota\varsigma$). Within the host he draws
a *natural* distinction, and assigns the deliberative func-
tions to the old, who have practical wisdom. The claim
'to rule and be ruled in turn' is thus satisfied in a
way; the young warriors will mature into counsellors.
The old Greek idea of $o\iota$ $\gamma\acute{\epsilon}\rho o\nu\tau\epsilon\varsigma$ (the elder men)—the
idea of authority going with age, which is also said to
be implied in the words 'eorl' (elder) and 'ceorl'
(younger man), is thus maintained by Aristotle.

The city in which Aristotle's burghers are to live is
to be fortunate in respect of situation. All the land must
be easily surveyed from its burg, and the territory
must lie fairly towards the sea, and be hard of access to
foes. The town itself should face the east and 'take
the morning' and the morning air. There should be
springs of well water, and the houses should be built

on several places of strength. The old arrangement of
narrow labyrinthine streets was safer in war, but the
new regular fashion of laying out a town which Hippodamus applied to the Piræus, leaving old Athens κακῶς
ἐῤῥυμοτομημένη διὰ τὴν ἀρχαιότητα, is fairer and more
commodious.[64] The two plans may be combined. Walls
there must surely be, and means of encountering the
new artillery and machines of war, while guard-
towers on the walls will be occupied by members of the
various messes. On a farseen height will be placed the
common halls of the magistrates and priesthood, and
close under their eyes the meetingplace of the freemen, not to be profaned by buying and selling. Near
by will be the gymnasia of the elders, but at a
distance the market-place and seats of the money-
changers, and close to the mart the messroom of the
magistrates who see to police and decide in suits about
contracts.

Now the citizens who are to dwell in this ideal city,
and be like the inhabitants of the Isles of the Blessed,
will above all men need to practise philosophy, temperance, justice. Other States either do not school their
people in these qualities or only in the two last, so far as
they go to make up martial virtue. Thus the Spartans have rusted in disuse, in spite of their attention to
training, and have even been defeated in war, and lost
th empire for which they toiled. Aristotle has chosen
citizens of a noble nature, and now wishes Reason to
mould that nature, through education and habit, into a
fitness for the virtuous leisure which is the crown of

[64] Dicæarch. Fragm. 140.

life. Arguing from his own psychology he proposes to educate the body first, then the passions, then the intellect, as each severally developes. Then follow a variety of minute precepts concerned with the breeding of children, the age of marriage, and restraints on population. These are almost as strange to modern usage and sentiment as the precepts of Plato were to Aristotle and the contemporaries of Aristotle. We are scarcely concerned with the sensible rule that babies should be allowed to cry as much as they like, and unhappily we have only a fragment of the Aristotelian theory of education, after the boy, at the age of seven, is removed from the care of women. The early education is mainly corrective; the child is to see and hear nothing slavish or impure, to listen to none of the foul tales, and behold none of the fouler orgies, of heathenism. From the age of seven to fourteen, and from fourteen to twenty-one, the youthful citizens are to be subjected to a public and uniform system of schooling, of which Sparta alone gave an example. As the End of the city is one, so shall its training be one in gymnastics, music, letters, and design. No study is to be specialised; gymnastic shall not make the lads brutal, as in Sparta, nor music make them professionals. Like Plato, and like the Pythagoreans, Aristotle recognises that music has a moral quality and influence on character. He denounces the new music, with its 'wonderful feats,' and praises the educational music, of which Plutarch says that the Greeks had lost the secret. We find this theory hard to understand, even if we remember that the harmonies revealed in music appeared to the Pythagoreans the mystic echo of the *correspondences* of Nature. Again, both Aristotle and Iamblichus in his Life of Pythagoras speak of the healing power (ἰατρεία) of music in a way which may be derived partly from old ideas about magical chants, partly from the study of instances like that of Saul. Thirdly, in early Greece, words, dance, and music went together, and could not be divided, so that to introduce new music meant the introduction of new words in place of sacred hymns, new dances, and perhaps new gods to be worshipped in the new fashion. We know that Aristotle would have retained some music for its moral effect, and more varied strains for mere delight in leisure. For the rest, his ideal State is left incomplete, because the portion of his work is lost in which he describes the education which should 'constrain and direct youth towards the right reason which the law affirms.' [65]

XIII.

LAND-TENURE IN GREECE.

IN writing of the State of Greece before the συνοίκισις, or establishment of the city, it has been said that when the Greeks still lived in villages, their land-tenure was probably like that of other early village communities. Reasoning merely from analogy, we should expect to find that the village life in Greece, like the village life in India, in Russia, in early England, in Java, among the Arabs, and so on, implied, at first, the communal

[65] Laws, 659, 660.

tenure of land. Each house-father would have his own
enclosure round his homestead, the beginning of several
property in land. This spot would be his very own, and
within the sacred ἕρκος the will of the father would be
law. Each householder would share with his kinsmen
of the village, in the right to till his equal portion of
the arable land of the village, to cut wood in the forest,
and to feed his cattle on the common pasture. In very
distant times it is probable that the lots of arable land
were shifted at stated or uncertain periods, as population varied, and as one part of the territory was
left fallow, and others taken in due rotation into
culture. On this system there would be no several
property except the enclosure, the tûn or ἕρκος. It is
probable, however, that, as certain husbandmen acquired
greater skill than their fellows in agriculture, they
would object to the constant repartition of the soil; [66] to
them, as to the Russian peasants now, the partition
would seem *le partage noir*. They would urge that
they had improved their plot, and that the system of
repartition was unjust to their skill, and expenditure
of time, manure, and labour. As this view would probably be pressed by the more powerful men of the village, it would result in a *permanent* partition of the
arable land. This partition would be in intention
equal, but it is likely that some families of distinction would absorb more than their equal share. At all
events, supposing such a division to have been made, it
is pretty clear that land and freedom would go together.

[66] Stubbs, Constitutional History of England, i. 52; Laveleye, De
La Propriété, p. 13.

The *ethel* means both the plot of land and the freedom,
and in contrast with the state of landless men, the
nobility, of the landowner. This process of development of land-tenure, or something like this, is so
general a fact in history that we should be tempted, *à
priori*, to conclude that it occurred among the Greeks,
even if we found no surviving traces of it in the early
laws of Greece.

If it is possible to hold this view of the early state
of land-tenure in Greece, many questions which are now
obscure may be answered with some plausibility, and
the answer, even if vague, will be at least intelligible.
The traditions of a golden age, when there was not

> fixus in agris
> Qui regeret certis finibus arva, lapis,

will seem to be more than a dream of poets. We shall
partly understand the origin of the tradition of the
Lycurgean repartition of the soil of Sparta; we shall
have some notion of the real condition of the Athenian
husbandmen whom Solon relieved from debt; and we
shall see that the early lawgivers, who decreed that the
lot of land should never be sold, and that Aristotle and
Plato, in making full citizenship depend on possession
of the soil, had facts of early history to support their
laws and back their theories.

Before going on to such conclusions we must notice
some valuable opinions on the other side of the question. M. Fustel de Coulanges, in his work on 'La
Cité Antique,' writes that 'the populations of Greece
and Rome from the earliest periods always recognised

private property in land. There never was a time when the soil was in common use, and we find no trace of the German system of annual partition.' [67] Again, Mr. Cox, in his 'History of Greece,' brings his acquaintance with Aryan customs to bear on the question: 'All the conditions of primitive Aryan society were, as we have seen, unfavourable to, if not altogether inconsistent with, the equal subdivision of real property.' [68]

A different view is that of Sir Henry Maine: 'There appears to be no country inhabited by an Aryan race in which traces do not remain of the ancient periodical redistribution;' and 'the original distribution of arable land was always into exactly equal portions corresponding to the number of free families in the township,' and 'the periodical redistribution ended in perpetuity.' [69] It is our object to show that the early lawgivers of Greece either lived in a time when the almost sacred tenure of the family lot, now held in perpetuity, was being broken up, or that they looked back to the tradition of such a time, and tried to restore it.

The traces of any preceding epoch of periodical redistribution are extremely faint. It existed among some of the islands, where it might be explained away as a vestige of Pelasgian practice. It is hinted at by Aristotle as having survived at Tarentum, but the reference is very doubtful. [70] Some authors see in the very ancient common meals, or συσσίτια, the record of a time when land was cultivated in severalty, and the produce divided; as Aristotle says, 'certain of the

---

[67] La Cité Antique, p. 62.   [68] History of Greece, i. 80.
[69] Maine's Village Communities, pp. 81, 82.   [70] Pol. vi. 5, 10.

barbarians use.' Again, there is the fact that, when a piece of land was sold at Thurii each of the neighbours who was a witness was paid a small piece of money, as if the community had once possessed a right in the land, for which they now received a nominal satisfaction. This would be the survival from a time when, as in Hindostan, the village community had veto on the sale of property.[71] These are but slight hints of communal property, and we would not press the re-equalisation (ἀνομάλωσις) of Phaleas; but the traces of an early and equal division *in perpetuity* are more convincing.

Much the most famous instance of an early equal division of soil is the redistribution attributed by Plutarch to Lycurgus. Mr. Grote has shown how many difficulties are involved in this story as it has reached us.[72] Whenever we have an authentic record of Sparta at all, we find the complaint that 'wealth makes the man,' and that there are extremes of riches and poverty. It need not follow, to be sure, that wealth is equal where arable land is equally divided; but Mr. Grote shows how very vague and untrustworthy is the tradition even of a redistribution.

M. Laveleye, on the other side, appears to think that though this *re*-distribution cannot be properly attributed to Lycurgus, yet there remained a tradition

---

[71] Laveleye, op. cit. 164, 165; Stubbs, Constit. Hist. i. 85; Senchus Mor. iii. 53.

[72] Grote, ii. 530–540; Hermann's Lehrbuch der Griechischen Antiquitäten, vol. i. p. 146 (ed. 1874). 'Lykurg hatte eine gleiche und bleibende Vertheilung des gesammten Grundeigenthums in eine Anzahl untheilbarer und unveräusserlicher Loose angeordnet.'

of an original equal distribution which was attached to the name of the great lawgiver.[73] In support of the existence of such a tradition he quotes Plato ('Laws,' 684). M. Laveleye's words are: ' We may pretty confidently discern the part of tradition and legend. There was an almost equal distribution of land (ἰσότητα τινά) in the Dorian invasion—that is, the part of history. (See Plato, 'Laws,' 684.) But the repartition of territory attributed to Lycurgus is the part of legend.' It may be doubted, however, whether the words ἰσότητα τινὰ refer to the Dorian conquerors, though Hermann also relies on this text. Again, Plato need not be quoting a tradition, he may be framing a hypothesis. So far we are entirely in the dark as to what really happened. A legend of a re-distribution made by Lycurgus, a legend not noticed by our earlier authorities, does not so much as prove that there existed a tradition of an equal distribution made at the time of the Dorian Conquest.

It is therefore curious to find Müller saying in his history of the Dorians, that ' the united testimony of all authors proves that the property of the Spartans was set out in equal lots,' and that this division was in strictness only a lower grade of community of property.[74]

In the midst of this confusion there is one certain and important fact. The number of full citizens of Sparta had once been eight or nine thousand, and in the time of Aristotle it had dwindled to one

---

[73] Laveleye, op. cit. 161, 162, cf. note.
[74] Müller, Dorians, ii. 200.

thousand. Coincident with this decline of the numbers of full citizens was the concentration of real property in few hands. There had been an age when eight
or nine thousand Spartans had land enough to provide
for their subscriptions to the common meals, which subscription was the ὅρος τῆς πολιτείας. If we allow then
eight or nine thousand lots for these eight or nine thousand men, and allow for the pasture land, forests, and
wastes, as well as for the property of the Periœci, it is
probable that very little arable ground was left over
in Laconia to form estates going much beyond the
limit of equality. There need not have been absolute equality of extent or value. The royal demesne
may have been large, but there must have been a
nearer approach to equality than Mr. Grote would
allow at the time when Sparta was rich in full
citizens.[75] Mr. Grote has observed that, in very early
times, we hear of rich men and poor men in Sparta,
but it by no means follows that the rich had much
larger *lots* than the poor. Their greater wealth, if we
judge by the analogy of Celtic Ireland, may have lain
in cattle, pastured on the common pasture ground,
which is not said to have been meted out at all, and
which certainly was not meted out among the
Germans.[76]

Again, Aristotle says that Plato would need a limit-

---

[75] Grote, ii. 557. Compare Müller, ii. 33, where the lots are certainly
large enough.

[76] For Spartans rich in cattle, compare Athenæus, iv. 141, and
for wealth in heroic times, Odyssey, xiv. 96, 104. The lot offered as
a rich reward to Meleager was a τέμενος of fifty acres, in the plain of
Calydon. Iliad, ix. 579.

less territory, 'Babylonian Lands,' to support his 5,000 idle citizens. But the soil of Sparta supported, at one time, more than 5,000, and there must have been only a small margin of land left for the larger estates which the noblest families and the king might manage to secure. Thus, on the whole, we find more than what Mr. Grote calls 'possible exaggeration of a small fact' in the late traditions of early equality of landed estates in Sparta. We have both the fact that many thousands of citizens had a sufficiency of land, and again, we have the analogy of other equal divisions of land by most early conquering peoples. It is therefore possible that the confused traditions of equality may have been a refraction from the past, as M. Laveleye suggests, perverted into an account of a Lycurgean redistribution, rather than, as Mr. Grote holds, a myth suggested by the desires of the disenfranchised citizens at the time of Agis. At the least, we may say, that if the original Dorian allotments were not equal, or nearly equal, the Dorian Conquest was an exception to what Sir Henry Maine calls a very general law.

We must remember, too, that land might in later times be concentrated in few hands without having been sold. The decay of Sparta showed itself in the disproportionate number of daughters born, and the kinsmen who married these daughters would fall heirs to the lots of the family whose males were extinct, and three generations of this sort of thing would make an immense difference in landed property.

EARLY LAND-TENURE IN ATTICA.

THE condition of land-tenure in early Attica is even more difficult to understand than in the case of Sparta. In Sparta, and in Dorian communities generally, we have the traces of an undoubted conquest; the land naturally falls into the hands of the conquerors, and they, in their contempt for husbandry, live on the rents paid by the vanquished peoples, who are reduced to various stages of servitude. But in Attica the people were proud of their immemorial freedom from invasion. It is only through the mists of mythology that we guess at a conquest in which the Ionians played the part of Dorians. When we come to times on the threshold of history, to the age of Solon, the land question is one of the chief social difficulties. We find an impoverished class of husbandmen, who seem to have been owners of the land, because we hear much of the mortgages on their estates; and, again, we read of ἐκτημόριοι, apparently tenant farmers, who paid either a sixth as rent, or who only kept a sixth of the produce of their farm for themselves. Now the Helots paid a fifth of the produce to their Spartan lords, and there seems nothing so very crushing in the contribution of a sixth, as to account for the distress of Athenian farmers, while it is impossible to suppose that the cultivators could afford to retain only one-sixth, and to take all the expenses of husbandry. Who then, in the first place, were the landlords of the ἐκτημόριοι? Boeckh says the Hopletes possessed all the land, in which case the mortgages prove that many of the Hoplete class were indebted to others in the same rank. There must apparently have been both small and large holders, and it is usual to suppose that the Eupatridæ were the large holders. Now some writers, as Dr. Curtius, make the Eupatridæ include all the 360 clans divisible into 10,800 houses.[77] As this number of full citizens is at least as great as the highest number ever attributed to Sparta, we return to the old difficulty: there could scarcely have been any land left for large estates, owned by the oligarchy. This view also seems to imply that clansmen and Eupatridæ are interchangeable terms, an idea disclaimed by Dr. Curtius in his appendix. We hear in point of fact of clans of no consideration.[78] Again, we find a doubt whether the Eupatridæ were autochthonous, or, on the other hand, foreign houses of distinction.[79] Perhaps the easiest way to understand the whole position is to remember that the συνοίκισις of Athens was a gathering together of several towns, not of villages. Each town must have had its own clans, and it is consistent with analogy to suppose that one of the clans in each town was that in which the blood of the race was supposed to run purest—was the royal clan from which rulers were chosen.[80] When Theseus united all the towns, Plutarch says [81] that he chose out and set apart the kingly clans of each from the yeomen and the labourers. To such Eupatridæ, as to Laertes in

[77] Curtius, vol. i. pp. 307, 476, 478 (Engl. Transl.).
[78] γένη ἄδοξα. Etym. Mag. 760, ap. Meier do Gent. Att. p. 10.
[79] Suidas *in verb.*
[80] Maine, History of Early Institutions, p. 132.
[81] Plutarch, Theseus, 25. πρῶτος ἀποκρίνας χωρὶς εὐπατρίδας καὶ γεωμόρους καὶ δημιουργούς.

Homer, it would be a discreditable thing to live in the country. But these noble houses would not include more than a small proportion of the members of γένη, who would still, very likely, stick by their original lots in the country. Everything would tend, however, to raise the town dwellers in wealth and culture; indeed, the very fact of chiefship implies wealth; and if we may look on Solon's law prohibiting the acquisition of landed property beyond a certain extent, as a trace of an old inalienability of lots, we may guess that the town nobles had begun to covet more than their mere lot of land. Now let us suppose that though the nobles' *lots* were originally little larger than those of other members of clans, yet that the nobles were wealthier in *cattle*; let us consider the absolute necessity of a large stock of cattle for rude agriculture; and we can understand that the Eupatridæ might allot some of their superfluous stock, on onerous conditions of rent, to free but poor landholders of the clans.[82]   We find this kind of tenure, where land was easily obtained, but the means of tillage was hard to get, producing various grades of debt and of clientship in early Ireland.[83] 'In very early times land was a drug, while capital was extremely perishable, added to with the greatest difficulty and lodged in very few hands.' Thus, while the *land* was the tenant's, he was obliged to take capital (cattle) from the chief, and if he took much was a *daer*, or scarcely free man, paying heavy rent, if he took little, a *saer* tenant, paying less rent, for stock, not for land.

---

[82] 'Need of many oxen.'   Nasse, Land Community, p. 43.
[83] Maine's Hist. of Early Institutions, *passim*.

For chiefs read Eupatridæ; for saer and daer men
of their clans read free γεωμόροι; and we have an intelligible account of how the poverty, debt, and servile
condition of men who were still landowners arose in
Attica. It might be in such an age of the extreme
importance of cattle that the primeval Athenian law
against killing oxen was made. I should be inclined,
however, to refer this law, both in Attica and India, to
another cause. Be this as it may, the introduction of
money, not long before Solon's time, must have complicated matters, and the mortgage pillars may be conceived
of either as records of an early attempt on the part
of Eupatridæ to seize the clansmen's lots, or as records
of the amount of the mortgage, or of dues of food rent,
on the land, or on the produce. Meantime hirelings
(θητές), and broken men from other tribes, would have
their own grievances. There would be plenty of distress, but by the removal of the ὅροι by Solon, and
the consequent decline of what we may almost call the
seignorial rights of the Eupatridæ over the lots of the
freeholders, the land would be left in the small holdings
of the democratic age, when Alcibiades had but sixty
acres, and when only 5,000 citizens were *not* landowners.[84]

We have tried to account for the curious fact that
freeholders were crushed with rent, and yeomen with
debt due to nobles, on the principle of Sir Henry Maine,
that wealth was part of the essence of nobility, as,
indeed, early warfare tends to enrich the chief. We
have adopted his suggestion of a way in which the

---

[84] Bocckh, Public Economy of Athens, p. 486.

debt would be incurred—namely, by a Greek form
of the custom of taking stock (French *chaptel de
fer*, Scotch *steel-bow*), crossed by the conditions of
urban life, and by the introduction of money. And
we have seen that, unfortunate as they were, the
debtors might yet be landholders, and so their lands
might be covered with ὅροι, *i.e.* pillars registering
rent on the land, or recording mortgage, if we suppose
that land was becoming alienable at least to the chiefs.
This theory supposes that ὅροι was as much the legal
name for mortgage pillars in Solon's time as in later
Athens.[85] Mr. Cox has recently tried to show that the
pillars were sacred land-marks which ' it was sacrilege to
touch.' As he also holds that the land *belonged* to the
Eupatridæ, it is not easy to understand why Solon removed the pillars, and how he dared to do so. If he
' freed the land ' in the sense that he gave it away, to
the previously non-holding cultivators, this was an
ἀναδασμός. Now we hear that the poor were annoyed
because he made *no* ἀναδασμός. If, on the other hand,
he only removed restrictions on the sale of land, how
did that benefit the 'impoverished cultivators'? It
was *rich* men, friends of Solon, who borrowed money and
bought up land, if we are to believe Plutarch. The money
they repaid after the depreciation of the currency ; the
land which, when they bought it, had rent or mortgage
on it, became after the *seisachtheia*, ἄστικτος, free from
ὅροι, or record-pillars. But the whole business is unintel-
ligible if we suppose Solon to have sacrilegiously removed

   [85] Harpocration, *s. v.* ; Cox, History of Greece, i. 201 ; Plutarch,
Solon, 16.

ancient and sacred land-marks. Things scarcely grow clearer when the historian says that the peasant, in the circumstances he has described, must either have become a free owner of the soil or have fallen back into his original subjection; and in the next sentence represents his peasant, presumably now a free owner, as still paying a rent. To whom this rent was paid, if the ownership of the Eupatridæ disappeared with their pillars —and if it did not disappear, why were the pillars removed—it is hard to say. Did the State resume all landed property?

In support of the theory that in early times the Greek freemen held almost equal lots of land, a number of facts in early legislation may be quoted from the 'Politics' of Aristotle. 'Men of old time,' he says, 'seem to have recognised the advantage of equality of property.' Thus, Solon laid down a law, which was common in other states, that there should be a maximum and limit to the acquisition of landed property.[86] Again, there was the injunction, as far as possible, τοὺς παλαιοὺς κλήρους διασώζειν. Philolaus gave the same law, described as peculiar to his legislation, to the Thebans.[87] In Thurii the nobles (γνώριμοι) broke the law of the state by acquiring all the land. *In the ancient states 'the first lots' could not be sold.* All the Aphytæans were landholders. Oxylus forbade lending on landed security. All these attempts to restrict the sale of land, and to keep it parcelled

---

[86] Pol ii 7, 6.

[87] Thurii; cf. Pol. v. 7, 9; Philolaus, Pol. ii. 12. Oxylus could not have forbidden the lending of *money*, which came in after his time.

out in small lots, may be taken, without much im-
prudence, as survivals of early custom. Plato, in
the regulations as to land-tenure in the 'Laws,' would
have returned to the old usage, by way of rendering his
community prosperous, free, and stationary.[88]   In short,
the views of property of the theorists in late Greece,
like the economical views of some modern writers,
were an attempt to restore an institution of which
the religious and family sanction had long been ob-
solete.

XIV.

THE ORIGIN OF SOCIETY.

' The hole of the pit whence we were digged.'

In dealing with the problems presented by the earliest
associations of men, Aristotle had two great advantages.
In the first place, Greek religious tradition on the
matter of the origin of society, and of the family, was
various and shifting, and bound the enquirer to no par-
ticular orthodoxy.   In the second place, Aristotle had
never heard of the Aryan race, and was not tempted to
imagine that one branch of the human stock enjoyed
some peculiar privileges, or grew up in a different way
from that by which the other families of man have been

[88] Plato, Laws, 740, 638, 684.

led towards civilisation.[89] In spite of this absence of
misleading notions, and in spite of his acquaintance with
the rude forms of kinship through women, or of mere
gregarious herding together, which observers like
Herodotus had noted among the Massagetæ and
Agathyrsi, 'the most delicate of mortals,' Aristotle con-
ceives of the family as the original unit of society.[90]
Many ages of this sacred institution have made the conception of the family so familiar that it is certainly
difficult to believe that there was a time our ancestors
were unacquainted with it, in its present form.   That
such a state of society may exist, however, experience
suggests.[91] The more minutely we examine the society of savages, the more clearly do we detect a
very gradual progress from kindred through females
only, to the patriarchal stage of family life, and so
to the family as we understand it.[92]   Now if the
nameless ancestors of the ancient Greeks ever passed
through the savage state, the inference would plainly
be that they too had gone through several stages

[89] Maine, Early History of Institutions, p. 96. 'It is to be hoped
that contemporary thought will before long make an effort to emanci-
pate itself from those habits of levity in adopting theories of race.'
[90] Herodot. iv. 104–172 ; Libyans, Pol. ii. 1, 13. The Family, Pol. i.
1, 5.
[91] McLennan, Primitive Marriage, p. 176.
[92] Morgan, Systems of Consanguinity and of Affinity, p. 469. 'The
evidence from the classificatory system tends to prove that marriage
between single persons was unknown to the primitive ages of mankind.'
Mr. Morgan's theory differs somewhat from that of Mr. McLennan. But
the connection between the higher and lower forms of kinship may be
traced by so many survivals, especially by the ceremony of capture, and
by nobility going on the female side, that I cannot share the doubts of
Sir Henry Maine (Early History of Institutions, pp. 66, 67). See also
Giraud Teulon, 'Origines de la Famille.'

of kinship before they reached the perfect family life
which we find them enjoying as soon as we make their
acquaintance in Homer. Now as far as the traditions
of Hellas, and the common opinion of the Hellenes
went, they had evolved their civilisation out of a condition of savagery. Both Aristotle and Plato, to go no
further, speak of the earliest men as 'earth-born,' or as
being the remnant of another race left after some deluge,
'small sparks of humanity preserved on the tops of
mountains.' 'Of cities, or governments, or legislation,'
they could have no idea at all.[93] Neither Plato nor
Aristotle, however, lays much stress on the nature of
their family arrangements; the latter says that 'the
Greeks of old used to buy their wives from each
other;' the former quotes the well-known passage from
the Odyssey about the Cyclopes 'giving laws each to
his own wife and children.' Thus the two philosophers
may be said to consider Greek life to have begun in the
patriarchal stage, where the father and house-master
has despotic power (*patria potestas*) over the members
of his household. In fact, Aristotle accounts for the
rise of kingly government in cities and tribes, by saying that these associations were made up of men who
had previously been accustomed to the kingly sway of
the paternal authority. Nor can there be much doubt
that the first Greeks who gathered into cities had long
been in the patriarchal stage, that each father had been
a king within his own ἕρκος, or house-enclosure, while
he was but a peer in the assembly of his village.

---

[93] Plato (Laws, 677-80; Pol. ii. 8, 21; Laws, 782) speaks of human
sacrifice, and of abstention from the flesh of the cow.

Without disputing this, we wish to ask if there was not
an age beyond the dawn of history, perhaps beyond the
dateless time when the common Indo-European terms
for father were coined, when the ancestors of the
Greeks knew no ties of blood at all, or knew them only
through females? Now, as we have said, the Greeks
themselves believed that such primitive simplicity had
once been their own condition. As a proof that they
accepted this view without the reluctance now so general, one might quote the words of Moschion, a late
writer of the school of Euripides:—

ἦν γάρ ποτ' αἰὼν κεῖνος, ἦν, ὁπηνίκα
θηρσὶν διαίτας εἶχον ἐμφερεῖς βροτοί ·
ὁ δ' ἀσθενὴς ἦν τῶν ἀμεινόνων βορά.[94]

This may be called a mere sophistic paradox; but the
author of the Homeric hymn to Hephæstus was no
sophist, and he speaks of men—

υἷ τὸ πάρος περ
ἄντροις ναιετάασκον ἐν οὔρεσιν ἠΰτε θῆρες.

It is only natural to attribute to cave-men the morality of cave-bears, and we shall see that Greek tradition did not scruple to do so. Cecrops, the *Serpent*
king of Athens, was credited with the invention of
marriage, as the Australian blackfellows of to-day
assign the innovation to the *Lizard*.[95]   Another legend

[94] I am indebted to Preller, Ausgewählte Aufsätze, p. 287.
[95] The words of Suidas are plain enough, p. 3102. πρότερον γὰρ αἱ
τῆς χώρας ἐκείνης γυναῖκες, κ.τ.λ. This and similar expressions are not
quoted as if they afforded any historical proof that such manners ever
prevailed among the tribes *settled in Greece*, but merely to show that
nothing in Greek feeling made belief in such a tradition impossible.

ran to the effect that, before Cecrops, children in Athens went by the mother's name, just as nobility went by the mother's side among the Lycians and Etruscans, just as 'the Picts chose their royal race ever on the mother's side,' just as nobility in heroic Greece came through the mother, and the Divine father who saw the daughters of men that they were fair.[96]

We thus find that neither tradition nor opinion in Greece ran absolutely counter to the view that Greeks had once been like barbarians, while barbarians had been like savages. It would not be hard to go further, and show that many traces in the symbolism of Greek marriage customs, that certain strange and revolting provisions of Greek law, are derived from an antiquity when the family was a very different thing from what it became in historic times. The mere persistence of a pretence of capture in the Spartan marriage ceremony points to a time when women had to be, as in so many Greek myths they were, stolen from a hostile tribe. And the fact that women had to be stolen points to the prohibition to marry within a man's own group, which again was deduced from a scarcity of women within the group, which must have made polyandry a necessity. To take another instance, the law which allowed an Athenian to marry his sister-german clearly looked on the relative by the father's side as no relative at all, while relationship on the *mother's* side was a sacred tie.[97] It is unnecessary to dilate on this subject

[96] The English Chronicle, p. 1.
[97] Plutarch, Solon.

more fully here, because Mr. McLennan has collected
enough of the evidence that makes for the ancient existence of kinship through women in Greece. What
we are now about to attempt is a mere application of
views which Mr. McLennan has originated and set
forth with an admirable combination of clearness,
originality, and learning.

There would perhaps be little reason to examine the
origin of the family in Greece if there were not grounds
for supposing that the process which ultimately developed the family produced also the germ of an association which lasted, as a political body, long after the
family had acquired its civilised form. This association
was the γένος; and the object of this essay is to contrast
the two views of the origin of that important political
factor, the views of Mr. McLennan and of Sir Henry
Maine. To state the matter shortly, we may say that
the former writer believes the γένος, or at least the germ
of the γένος, to have existed prior to the evolution of the
patriarchal family; while the latter, like Aristotle, Mr.
Freeman, Mr. Cox, Mr. Grote, and Mr. Kemble, holds,
or did hold, that the γένος was probably composed by
aggregation of families. By the first theory, the γένος
was the earlier unit, and the families grew up and separated each from each within the bosom of the group. By
the latter theory, the ordinary family existed first in
time, and the γένος was formed later by the extension of
the single family, and by the adoption of other families
into the first.[98]

---

[98] Early History of Institutions, p. 66; Freeman's Comparative
Politics, p. 104. Dicæarchus held the same view, if we suppose πάτρα

We have already seen the great political importance of the γένος in Greece. This association answered to the *gens* at Rome, and to the *sibsceaft*, or kinship, which, when settled within its own mark of land, is known in early Teutonic history as the *Markgenossenschaft*. Whether in Greece, Rome, or England, not to mention other countries, the members of each of these kinships all bore the same patronymic name, were all held together by the two most sacred bonds—of belief that they shared the same blood, and of participation in the same religious rites and worship of a heroic ancestor. Whether in Greece, England, or Rome, the chief families in these kinships, subordinated to the wider tribal arrangement, formed the earliest aristocracies. Outside the *gentes* there was neither tribal right, nor civic right, nor land, save at exorbitant rack-rent, for the stranger who settled in their neighbourhood. Even in the later times of Greece, full citizenship generally implied admission within the sacred circle of gentile feasts and sacrifices. The question which we have now to ask is, did the members of each γένος really partake in any degree of common blood; were they really kindred, or was the idea of kinship little more than a legal fiction? That any traceable blood connection had disappeared in the time of Pericles, or of Gracchus, may be admitted at once. Indeed, there was a definition which recognised the γεννῆται as connected by

---

to have the same meaning as γένος. φρατρία, with him, is the union on festal occasions (ἱερῶν κοινωνικὴ σύνοδος) of brothers and sisters, who have married into different πάτραι. φυλὴ, or tribe, is a still later and larger division after the σύνοδος εἰς τὰς πόλεις.—Dicæarch. Fragm. 139.

THE ΓΕΝΟΣ FOUNDED ON KINSHIP. 97

customary law (νόμῳ), as having been ἐξ ἀρχῆς εἰς τὰ καλούμενα γένη κατανεμηθέντες. In several places the γεννῆται are defined as οὐχ οἱ ἐκ γένους καὶ ἀφ’ αἵματος προσήκοντες. Gentile relations, then, were not necessarily, or at least in later times could not make out that they were, blood relations.[99] The ancient tie of kindred had come to be thought part of some consciously invented division of the citizens, but it cannot be doubted that long before the beginning of political legislation the γένη had grown up out of some real ties of blood. The right to share in the property of a deceased fellow gentile, the duty ðf taking up the blood feud for him if he were slain, the common burying-place, sufficiently prove that kinship was at the bottom of the gentile division.

How, then, did the γένος come into existence? Now, if we allege, with Sir Henry Maine, ' that it is difficult to say of what races of men it is *not* allowable to lay down that the society in which they are united was originally organised on the patriarchal model,' we must accept the usual theory of the origin of the γένος.[100] We must say, with Mr. Freeman, that ' the family grew into the clan, and the clan grew into the tribe.' We must say, with Mr. Cox, that though the father of the

[99] See a number of extracts in Meier, De Gent. Att., showing that the lexicographers supposed the gentile relationship to have been produced by enactment, νόμῳ τινὶ ἔχοντες κοινωνίαν. The synonyms for near kin, such as ὁμογάλακτες (collactanei), ὁμόσιπνοι, ὁμοκάπνοι, quoted by Aristotle from early authorities, like Charondas and Epimenides, correspond to 'Gaelic teadhloch and coedhichc, meaning, the first, having a common residence, the second, those who eat together.' (M'Lennan, Primitive Marriage, p. 154.) They certainly seem to base kinship rather on milk ties and residence than on blood affinity.
[100] Ancient Law, p. 132.

H

primitive household 'knew nothing of ritual common to other families,' and though the 'primitive Aryan' lived 'in utter isolation,' yet that 'the original families might combine for the purpose of extending their power and increasing it.' It is very hard to see how this union of hostile *families* into *tribes* was brought about. Mr. Cox is led to suppose that the primitive Aryan lived 'in lawful wedlock,' in a den 'which, save his mate and offspring, no other living thing might enter, except at the risk of life.' We must presume that after his death the primitive Aryan became 'the god' of his children, that his younger sons became the heads of new families, which were kept in strict subordination to the chief who, in the direct line, represented the original progenitor, and who thus became the king of a number of houses, that is, of a tribe.[101] This view, which is shared by M. Fustel de Coulanges, is a perfectly simple, clear, and natural one; but how far is it based on history, how far is it based on the facts of primitive life? No real explanation seems to be given of the fact that families, said to be *exclusive* both by brute instinct and by selfish religion, *combined* with other families equally exclusive. Yet there is no doubt at all that distinct families were combined in the local tribes. The original exclusiveness could scarcely have been overcome, as Mr. Cox suggests, by any far-sighted policy of 'extending and increasing the power' of families that, *ex hypothesi*, detested each other. Again, if we suppose the original family to have merely increased and multiplied into a

[101] Cox's History of Greece, vol. i. pp. 15, 16.

homogeneous tribe, why were the local tribes *not* homogeneous? why were they local aggregates of clans of *different* patronymics and different religions? There is still another difficulty. How is it that, among nations still in the clan stage of society, we find the same *family* names prevailing in different and distant *local tribes*? Take the case of Australia, one finds the same *family* names, scattered through the different *local tribes* all over the continent. Take the case of early England, one finds the traces of the clan of Billingas in Northampton, Lancashire, Durham, Lincoln, Yorkshire, Sussex, Salop, and other widely separated districts.[102] Here, then, are three difficulties—first, that of accounting for the *non-homogeneous* character of local tribes if they sprang from *one* kinship; secondly, the difficulty of accounting for the *union* of elements confessedly so *exclusive* as the different families; thirdly, of understanding how the same *family* names were scattered through many *local tribes*. The last question scarcely meets the student of Greek and Roman history, but it at once encounters the reader of early English history, and the observer of existing societies still in the tribal and clan stage of civilisation.

Sir Henry Maine solves the first problem, that of the non-homogeneous character of local tribes, by supposing that one family admitted others within its circle by the legal fiction of adoption. 'The expedient was that the incoming peoples should feign themselves to

---

[102] Kemble's Saxons in England, vol. i. p. 458; M'Lennan, Primitive Marriage, pp. 273, 274, and Sir George Grey's 'Journals,' vol. ii. p. 227.

be descended from the same stock as the people on whom they were ingrafted.' [103]   Mr. M'Lennan asks, 'where is the evidence that the fiction of adoption was ever employed on so large a scale as to account for the heterogeneity of such groups as the tribes of Rome, Greece, or India?' One might point, in reply, to the very modern instance of the Kaffirs. Within the memory of men a certain Englishman has become the nominal father of a tribe of more than three thousand Kaffirs. This came about through a curious kind of savage 'commendation.' The English settler, who was rich in cattle, bought wives for a number of Kaffir vassals; these vassals took his family name as a tribal name; they increased and multiplied, holding their wives of the Englishman on condition of military service, and our countryman, a Mr. Finn, is thus the nominal father of the whole tribe of Ama-Finns. There must meanwhile be numerous older family names within the tribe of Ama-Finns. Here is a bizarre instance of the extension, by adoption and legal fiction, of the Finn family. Curious as this case of adoption seems, it is not an example of the process by which family names got scattered through the local tribes over the continents of Australia and North America, and, as it seems, over North Germany in the ages before the English invasion of Britain.

There is good reason to believe that the γένη of Greece, the Roman gentes, the *sibsceafts* of the early English, were not developed out of the family as we understand it, by natural increase and by adoption.

[103] Ancient Law, pp. 130, 131.

They were very probably survivals from an earlier stage of kinship than that of the ordinary family. It was not the processes of natural increase of one family, and of adoption into it, that developed the clans of Australia and of North America. The members of these clans bear each the clan patronymic, perform the same superstitious rites, and are bound to mutual defence. So far they resemble the Greek γένη. Again, they are scattered through all the local tribes, so that, in Australia, a man of the Kangaroo *family* may belong to the Waddaroke local tribe, or to the Ballarat *local tribe*, and so on, just as in England a man of the Billinga clan, or of the Arlinga clan, might be a Somersaeta, or a Huicca, or a Lindisfara by local tribe. This curious scattering of the *family* names through the *local* settlements in England has puzzled Mr. Kemble, who accounts for it by the confusion of the English invasion, and by later wanderings and colonisations. But if the Arlingas, Billingas, and so forth, were once scattered over North Germany, as the men of the Snake, Sun, or Tortoise clans are scattered all over America and Australia, it would necessarily happen that when a Jutland tribe invaded the south of England, it would leave families settled there of the same names as a Schleswig tribe would leave in the north or west of England.[104]

Now, it can be absolutely proved that the clans of America and Australia were developed not out of aggregations of ordinary families, but through counting kindred by the *female* side, and through a strange custom which prohibits a man from marrying a woman

[104] Kemble's Saxons in England, vol. i. p. 59.

of his own patronymic. 'The children take after the
clan of the mother, and no man can marry a woman of
the same clan, though the parties be in no way related
according to our ideas.' [105] We have seen that the
members of the γένος were ' in no way related according
to our ideas,' οὐ κατὰ γένος ἀλλήλοις προσήκοντες οὐδ'
ἀπὸ τοῦ αὐτοῦ αἵματος, according to their later notions
of relationship.

If we trace the results of the savage rule of marriage, we see that a man of the Ballarat tribe, and of
the Swan family, may not marry a Swan woman. If
he marries a woman of the Wandyalloch tribe, and of
the Kangaroo family, his children, taking *her* name,
become Kangaroos within the Ballarat local tribe and
almost within the Swan γένος. Yet they are bound to
fight, in case of blood feud, for the Kangaroo family in
whatever local tribe it may be situated. Thus, by a
process not that of adoption, one family, however naturally hostile to all other families, is brought within their
circle. It is scarcely necessary to trace the causes of the
two primitive marriage rules, the one prohibiting marriage with a woman of one's own family name, the
other making children take the mother's family name,
as tradition says that they did in early Athens. It
is enough that these rules account for the heterogeneity of local tribes, for the existence of γένη which
have a tradition of kinship, though no real kinship is
traceable, and for the dispersion of these all through
distant localities. As to the causes of these marriage

[105] The Aboriginals of Australia, G. Scott Lang, p. 10; Primitive
Marriage, p. 113; Morgan, Systems of Affinity, p. 149.

OBJECTIONS. 103

rules, they hold of conduct which Sir Henry Maine con-
templates when he speaks of practices which 'it would
be unjust and incorrect to call immoral, because . . . .
they are older than morality.' These causes produced
the savage groups of America and Australia—the question is whether the γένη of Athens, the gentes of Rome,
and the English *sibsceaft* are but traces of practices
'older than morality' in the Aryan race.

Against this view it may be urged that the Australians and American Indians are even now in the habit
of deriving family names through female kinship, which
the γένη of *historical* Greece did not do. But this
makes no difference to the argument. It is easy to
imagine the Australians beginning—the Indians have
already begun—to derive names through the father,
and to permit marriage between men and women bear-
ing the same name. When they do so—if the Aryan
settlers let them live till they do so—they will not alter
the fact that gentile families are scattered all over
Australia. The names and a tradition of kinship will
survive, just as the names with tradition of kinship
survived in various degrees in Greece, and Rome, and
England. The family grew up within the group by a
process of appropriation and of the development of individual claims. When it was fullgrown it seemed
prior in time to the group, whereas it was only prior
in idea, as the state, according to Aristotle, is earlier
than the family in idea.

Another very obvious objection to the theory that
the γένος is earlier than the family is perhaps of little
weight. The savage κοινωνίαι we have spoken of are

named after what are called Totems, by the names of
plants and animals, or of the sun, or water, or earth.
They reverence the vegetable, or beast, or natural force
from which they think they spring, and will rarely
pluck the plant or slay the beast. Now the English,
Greek, and Roman kinships deduced their stock from
some eponymous hero, not from a totem, and this difference in practice may seem to imply a difference in
the kind of association. But it may be conjectured
that a time must have come to Greeks and Teutons,
when tribes that had once believed in some tradition of
descent from beast, or bird, or fish found the notion
incredible. We know that the Zulus have reached this
stage of scepticism.[106] Such people would either look
on the old story as an allegory, and consider the Snake,
or the Sun, of their ancestors as a mere name for some
real man, or they would transfer their adoration from
the Totem to some distinguished chief of their stock,
whom they would 'seek to lord and to *Father*.' His
name would be the name of his clan, which would
thenceforth only bear the effigy of the bestial or animal
ancestor as a crest or banner in war. If we look at
Greek and Northern traditions with this in mind, we
may guess why the γένος of the Ioxidæ reverenced
asparagus, why many Attic demes were called after the
names of plants, why the Bear appears as an ancestor in
Scandinavian pedigrees, why the *boar* was the amulet
of the Scyldings, why there was a hero of the form of a
wolf at Athens.[107]

[106] Callaway's Religion of the Amazulu.
[107] Plutarch, Theseus, for the Ioxidæ. For the Bear, see Freeman,

The origin of the family is a question that has its disagreeable side. The painfulness of the study may be compensated if it teaches us to throw away the absurd pride of race, which furnishes so-called Aryans with a semi-scientific excuse for despising the 'lower races,' on account of practices that have left their mark in Aryan institutions.

Norman Conquest, i. 420; for the Boar, see Kemble's Beowulf and notes; for the Wolf-shaped hero, see Harpocration under δεκάζειν. Something in this direction might be made out from a philological analysis of the patronymics given in Mr. Kemble's Saxons·in England. Compare Grote, iii. 85, 'A great many of the demes seem to have derived their names from the shrubs and plants which grew in their neighbourhood,' with Sir G. Grey, ii. 228, 'One origin of family names frequently ascribed by the natives is, that they were derived from some vegetable or animal being common in the district which the family inhabited.'

www.ingramcontent.com/pod-product-compliance
Lightning Source LLC
Chambersburg PA
CBHW030547270326
41927CB00008B/1547